Yale Series in Economic History

Economic Opportunity and White American Fertility Ratios

1800–1860

by

COLIN FORSTER

and

G. S. L. TUCKER

With the assistance of Helen Bridge

New Haven and London : Yale University Press

1972

Designed by John O. C. McCrillis
and set in IBM Baskerville type.
Printed in the United States of America by
The Murray Printing Co., Forge Village, Massachusetts.

Published in Great Britain, Europe, and Africa by
Yale University Press, Ltd., London.
Distributed in Canada by McGill-Queen's University Press, Montreal;
in Latin America by Kaiman & Polon, Inc., New York City;
in Australasia and Southeast Asia by John Wiley & Sons
Australasia Pty., Ltd., Sydney; in India by UBS Publishers'
Distributors Pvt., Ltd., Delhi; in Japan by John Weatherhill,
Inc., Tokyo.

Contents

Tables and Figures

Preface

This study was provoked by Yasukichi Yasuba's *Birth Rates of the White Population in the United States, 1800-1860* (Baltimore: The Johns Hopkins Press, 1962). We have drawn heavily on some of his basic data and wish to express our thanks both to him and The Johns Hopkins Press for permission to do so.

We were assisted throughout by Helen Bridge, to whom we are deeply grateful. Although we had access to a computer and a programmed desk calculator, the sections using non-parametric methods in particular called for hard slogging on her part, there being few opportunities here to replace labor with capital equipment.

Miss M. Rose supplied programs for the computer. Members of the Department of Statistics, Faculty of Economics, were invariably patient and helpful in answering our many questions. Our thanks are due also to the Population Division of the U.S. Bureau of the Census for the tabulation of urban places and their populations referred to in chapter 5.

C.F.
G.S.L.T.

Faculty of Economics
The Australian National University

Introduction

At the beginning of the nineteenth century, the birth rate in the United States may have been as high as fifty to fifty-five per thousand; thus it exceeded those of western European countries for which estimates are available. Its trend thereafter was downward, and this again is a distinguishing feature of American demographic experience. In western Europe there may have been special cases such as France, where it is thought the birth rate probably was declining from the late eighteenth or early nineteenth century onward, but more typically the European pattern shows a roughly horizontal trend until the mid-nineteenth century or rather later, when the modern transition toward lower fertility began. All this is familiar.

It remains a problem, however, to explain the early decline of the American birth rate, occurring at a time when the economy was still mainly rural in character. As Coale and Zelnik have said: "The birth rate in the United States fell extensively—from 55 to 41 per thousand—between 1800 and 1860, while the population remained nearly 80 per cent rural. . . . To account for the decline in fertility in non-industrial environments would be a fruitful form of historical research."[1]

An analysis of this question was made recently by Yasukichi Yasuba in his *Birth Rates of the White Population in the United States, 1800-1860,*[2] which was described by a reviewer as a "fascinating book" of meticulous scholarship.[3] Dealing as it does with economic and social influences on fertility in a rapidly growing economy, Yasuba's work should be of considerable interest not only to demographers but also to all students of American economic history. Our purpose is to give a brief description of his methods and then to offer some further discussion of his view that in the early decades of the nineteenth century "a major determinant" both of geographical differences in fertility at any given time and of the general downward trend of fertility over time was the relative ease or difficulty

1

with which new land could be obtained in the settled areas for the creation of additional rural households.[4] (Yasuba allowed some weight also to the effects of industrialization-urbanization but assigned them "a major role" only after the middle of the century.) Writing on American population in a paper published in 1965, J. Potter has noted that this conclusion gave "more weight to the decrease in the availability of 'easily accessible land' in explaining the decline in fertility than to urbanization and industrialization," and he claimed that "the argument is not very convincing."[5] Our own feeling is that an accurate assessment of the force of Yasuba's thesis—intrinsically a most important one, if the conclusions it suggests are correct—calls for a much more extensive discussion than Potter has been able to undertake. For this reason we wish to look again at Yasuba's case.

1

Decline in Fertility: Yasuba's Analysis

It is convenient to use the word *fertility*, but Yasuba is forced
by deficiencies of data to adopt a measure which approximates
only roughly to this concept. This is the *birth ratio* (sometimes called a fertility ratio, age ratio, or child-woman ratio),
whose advantage is that it can be calculated directly for each
state or territory of the United States at all census dates during the period 1800-1860. It differs from the birth rate in
that it refers, not to numbers of births (which for these years
can be obtained only as estimates), but rather to the number
of children of less than a given age living at the time of a census.
Thus the "white refined birth ratio" is defined as the number
of children under ten years of age per 1,000 white women aged
sixteen to forty-four.[1] For the United States between 1800
and 1860 this fell from 1,844 to 1,308, or by 29.1 percent.

Unlike crude measures of fertility, the refined birth ratio
takes account of changes in the proportion of the total population consisting of women of childbearing age. However, age-
specific fertility ratios vary *within* the childbearing span, and
it is not wholly satisfactory simply to consider numbers of
women in the broad age group of sixteen to forty-four. Thus
for census years from 1830 onward (at which date there was
an improvement of age classification), several attempts have
been made to standardize the refined birth ratio to the age
distribution of women in a given year. Yasuba uses the age
distribution of 1860 and assumes a curve of age-specific birth
ratios of the general shape shown in the Thirteenth Census of
1910.[2] So far as differences of birth ratios between separate
states and territories were concerned, he found that "the
effect of the age-distribution was minor in most instances."
For the country as a whole, age distribution of women within
the childbearing span had changed over time in such a way as

to give an upward bias to the unstandardized refined birth ratio, whose fall, when standardized, turned out to be "somewhat greater."[3]

Downward trends of refined birth ratios are evident in the separate states and territories, as well as in the United States as a whole. Most of Yasuba's data of these ratios (unstandardized to 1820 and standardized from 1830 onward) are shown in figure 1, where they are grouped by census divisions.[4] While in some cases there were early periods during which birth ratios rose or remained nearly stable, the general characteristics of the long-run trends are similar. The interesting feature is that although the trends are downward, the initial levels of birth ratios vary as between different states. Thus the curves have different positions in relation to the vertical axis; for example, not only do the levels of curves for New England states differ *inter se,* lying bodily one below another, but also they all occupy lower positions than those for states of the more recently settled East North Central division. Similar comparisons could be made between levels of curves for states of the old-settled Middle Atlantic division and others for newer states and territories farther west. Taking cross sections of the data, we have *at any given point of time* an array of values for the refined birth ratios, and this opens up to Yasuba a possibility of applying methods of rank correlation in order to test hypotheses regarding the determinants of fertility.

Yasuba selects several hypotheses for investigation, two of which find a place in his final conclusions. These are, first, that levels of fertility, and hence refined birth ratios, depended on economic opportunities for the establishment of new households, for the relative plenty or scarcity of these opportunities in a state or territory could have affected the average age of women at first marriage, the proportions of women ever married, and the incentives of married people to restrict family sizes;[5] second, that fertility may have varied inversely with

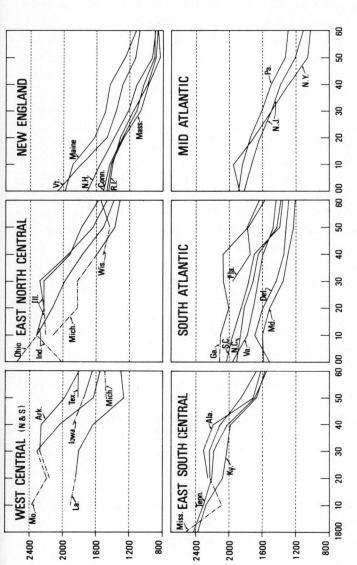

Figure 1. White refined birth ratio, by state or territory, census divisions, 1800-1860. Broken lines indicate periods during which there were significant changes of boundaries. Unstandardized refined birth ratios are shown prior to 1830 and standardized birth ratios thereafter.

Source: Yasuba, *Birth Rates*, tables 2.7 and 4.12, pp. 61-62 and 131-32.

urbanization and industrialization, which probably raised
the costs of bringing up children, reduced their value as
contributors to family income, increased the employment
opportunities of women, made available more competing
enjoyments, and facilitated the spread of knowledge. We
can look at these briefly in turn.

It seemed to Yasuba that opportunities for marriage and
the setting up of new households among the predominantly
rural population would have depended pretty largely (and
especially in the earlier part of the period) on the availability
of easily accessible land. Admittedly, there was always a
frontier where land was cheap, but "as time passed, the
acquisition of new land in the settled areas became increas-
ingly difficult and costlier and the average distance from
the settled to the new areas where land was plentiful became
farther. Consequently, fertility in the older communities
may have been reduced directly in response to the decreased
demand for children or indirectly as a result of the rise in the
age at marriage and the fall in the incidence of marriage."[6]
Thus we might expect refined birth ratios in different parts
of the country to vary inversely with the ratios of population
to arable land—more briefly, with what Yasuba calls "population density."

Ideally Yasuba would have liked to test this hypothesis
for areas as small as counties, but this would have called
for endless computations. The next best thing was to use the
states as units. For each state or territory at each census date
he computes population density or the number of persons
per 1,000 acres of arable land, the latter being defined, for
want of a better measure for the period in question, as cropland as of the year 1949. These state figures of population
densities are then ranked at each date and compared with the
ranking of state birth ratios. Results are summarized in his
table 5.10 (p. 165), reproduced here in table A.

Table A. Kendall's Coefficient of Rank Correlation (τ)
between the Number of Persons per 1,000 Acres
of Arable Land and the White Refined
Birth Ratio in a State or Territory:
United States, 1800-1860

	1800	1810	1820	1830	1840	1850	1860
For all states and territories†	-.633**	-.848**	-.802**	-.773**	-.675**	-.604**	-.526**
For free states and territories†	-.667*	-.927**	-.848**	-.879**	-.795**	-.633**	-.555**
For slave states and territories†	-.571	-.714*	-.673**	-.641**	-.560**	-.619**	-.583**

Note: Arable land is defined as cropland in 1949. The refined birth ratio
is the number of children under 10 years of age per 1,000 women aged
16-44. Standardized refined birth ratios are used for 1830 and later.

*Significant at the 5% level.
**Significant at the 1% level.
†Only those states and territories that had approximately the same area
in the year mentioned as in 1949.

In summary, Kendall's coefficient suggests a close inverse
association between fertility and population density, though
the successive decreases in its value after 1810 make it appear
that the association was tending to become weaker as time
passed. Yasuba concludes that "the extent of land-use within
the settled areas, or the availability of easily accessible land
nearby, may have been an important determinant of the
level of fertility throughout the period, 1800-1860, particularly in the early part of it."[7]

To test the second hypothesis relating to urbanization and
industrialization as determinants of fertility, Yasuba applies
similar methods of rank correlation to data of the urban
proportions of the populations of states and territories; and

also, as far as they can be measured, the proportions employed
in nonagricultural pursuits. Results for urban proportions
are summarized in his table 5.4 (p. 144), part of which is
reproduced here in table B, while those for proportions
employed in nonagricultural pursuits can be extracted from
his text (p. 156) and shown in a similar form (see table C).

Table B. Kendall's Coefficient of Rank Correlation (τ)
between the White Refined Birth Ratio and the
Proportion of Urban Population in a State or
Territory: United States, 1800-1860

	1800	1810	1820	1830	1840	1850	1860
For all states and territories	-.468*	-.360*	-.544**	-.409**	-.495**	-.593**	-.366**
For free states and territories	-.674*	-.587*	-.507*	-.427*	-.541**	-.553**	-.355*
For slave states and territories	-.261	-.024	-.556*	-.169	-.544**	-.708**	-.543**

*Significant at the 5% level.
**Significant at the 1% level.

Table C. Kendall's Coefficient of Rank Correlation (τ)
between the White Refined Birth Ratio and the
Proportion of Workers Employed in Nonagricultural Pursuits in a State or Territory

	1820	1840	1850	1860
For all states and territories	-.551**	-.655**	-.558**	-.621**

Note: The figure for the year 1860 is not given by Yasuba but has been
computed by us from his data.

*Significant at the 5% level.
**Significant at the 1% level.

Except in 1850, the inverse association between fertility
and the proportion employed in nonagricultural pursuits
is stronger than that between fertility and the proportion
of urban population; but, on the whole, neither is as close
as that between fertility and population density. The difference in favor of the latter is most pronounced in the earlier
part of the period. By 1850 the three coefficients of rank
correlation (computed for all states and territories) approach
equality, although the gap opens again in 1860 owing to a
sudden decrease in the coefficient of correlation between
fertility and the proportion of urban population. In general,
Yasuba concludes that "if industrialization-urbanization
played an important role in reducing fertility, it began to
do so only towards the end of the period, 1800-1860."[8]

Yasuba recognizes a difficulty of interpretation arising
from the fact that the numbers used to calculate population
densities per 1,000 acres of arable land (his measure of the
relative ease or difficulty of establishing additional rural
households) include those living in towns; or looked at from
the other direction, urbanization in a state or territory might
tend to be higher, the greater the scarcity of arable land and
so the more abundant the labor supply potentially available
for nonfarm occupations. Thus, when computed, there turns
out to be a significant positive association between population density and the urban proportion, and this becomes
closer toward the end of the period.[9] In effect, he is being
called upon to deal with a triad of related variables which
can be represented in the form:

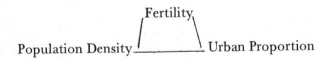

Population Density ———————— Urban Proportion

The problem, obviously, is to take account of the cross-correlation between the two variables postulated as determinants
of fertility.

Yasuba attempts to do so by means of his method of "standardized rank correlation" or "moving standardization," which is referred to in notes 7 and 8 to this chapter. Results are summarized in his table 5.13 (p. 174), part of which can be shown as in table D.

Table D. Coefficient of Rank Correlation between the White
Refined Birth Ratio and One of the Socioeconomic
Variables in a State or Territory, with States
and Territories Standardized with Respect
to the Other Socioeconomic Variable

Correlation between the refined birth ratio and:

	Population density†	Proportion of urban population††
1800	−.825	−.333
1810	−.806	−.250
1820	−.787	−.343
1830	−.705	−.214
1840	−.371	−.389
1850	−.510	−.391
1860	−.419	−.346

†When states and territories are standardized with respect to the proportion of urban population.
††When states and territories are standardized with respect to population density.

"Thus," he concludes, "it appears that population density, which, with states and territories standardized with respect to the degree of urbanization, presumably represents the availability of easily accessible land, was much more important than industrialization-urbanization as a factor affecting fertility during the first few decades of the nineteenth century. The importance of the former diminished with time, while that of the latter increased. Yet it was not until after the Civil War . . . that the relative importance of the two factors was reversed."[10]

2

Alternative Measures and Changes in Land Accessibility

Yasuba's statistical analysis is forceful and carefully conducted; moreover, his conclusion regarding the likely importance of the relative abundance or scarcity of easily accessible land as a determinant of fertility in the early decades of the nineteenth century seems to us, intuitively, to have more in its favor than the alternative thesis emphasizing the effects of urbanization. After all, for the country as a whole, the proportion of the population living in urban places did not rise above 10 percent until 1840, and while five eastern states and one southern had considerably higher urban proportions in that year,[1] reference to figure 1 shows that the falling tendency of refined birth ratios was much more widespread.[2] However, we feel there are some elements in his treatment that might tend to lessen the conviction it would otherwise have carried.

First, there is his use of the acreage of cropland *in 1949* to calculate population densities, and hence economic opportunities in agriculture, for the separate states and territories at census dates between 1800 and 1860. As he admits, this makes no allowance for the manner in which changes in agricultural techniques and transport facilities have altered the acreage of available land during the intervening period (*Birth Rates,* p. 161). Neither does cropland in 1949 reflect other factors such as the distribution of land ownership or the use to which land was put (*Birth Rates,* p. 168); it cannot distinguish between intensive and extensive farming and gives little indication of farming possibilities in animal husbandry. Again, this measure would seem much less appropriate in the southern than the northern states, because of the particular nature of the southern rural economy. Thus one of our objectives has been to find a measure of the availability

11

of easily accessible land, or economic opportunity in agriculture, which does something to reduce these uncertainties. This will be discussed in chapter 3.

Second, as Yasuba recognizes, results obtained by his method of "standardized rank correlation" or "moving standardization" (such as those in table D) cannot be tested for significance, since the variance of the coefficient is not known. Moreover, this deficiency could not be remedied by calculating Kendall's coefficient of partial rank correlation, which might alternatively have been used: perhaps Kendall's partial coefficient relies on less arbitrary methods than Yasuba's "moving standardization" and may be a better measure, but it has a similar weakness in that attempts to devise tests of significance for it have so far been unsuccessful.[3] Our second objective, therefore, has been to find a way around this difficulty at the point where it impinges most strongly on the analysis; that is, when we try to take account of the correlation between population density and the proportion of urban population—the two factors competing for pride of place as determinants of fertility—so as to obtain a measure of the partial association between the refined birth ratio of a state or territory and each of these variables. This will be attempted in chapter 4.

Third, there may be a further source of uncertainty connected with Yasuba's treatment of relative levels of urbanization in states and territories, since this does not consider interstate differences in the distribution of urban inhabitants by size of place. Possibly differences of this kind could affect the associations, as measured, between refined birth ratios and levels of urbanization, and hence, indirectly, the partial or "standardized" correlations between birth ratios and population densities, which are supposed to eliminate the influence of differences in urban proportions. Elaboration of this question will be deferred until chapter 5, which also contains an alternative analysis intended, as best we can, to deal with it.

Essentially, we have sought to work separately with the rural populations of states and territories and so to obtain direct measures of the relation between the *rural* refined birth ratio and "the availability of easily accessible land."

Finally, we believe that Yasuba's evaluation of the influence of one of the supposed socioeconomic determinants of fertility—population density—may have been affected to some extent by a more purely demographic factor, traceable to a selective element in internal migration. Again, it will be easiest at this stage simply to note the point, without attempting to develop it in detail. This will be undertaken later, in chapter 7, following a brief digression on intrastate fertility differentials to be given in chapter 6. Some aspects of the influence of immigration from Europe before the Civil War are discussed in chapter 8. Chapter 9 attempts to measure in a purely statistical sense the respective contributions to the total change in the national white refined birth ratio of (1) the decline in the rural refined birth ratio, (2) the decline of the urban refined birth ratio, and (3) the rural-to-urban shift of population.

For the moment, in the remainder of the present chapter, we wish to offer some comments intended to support the view that the "filling up" of the older states was a very real phenomenon, which in some circumstances could happen quite quickly, thus rapidly increasing (in Yasuba's words) "the degree of difficulty of obtaining new land not far from the place of residence" (*Birth Rates,* p. 160).[4] Of course, the general character of the westward expansion of American population is well known, and clearly this movement might be interpreted to imply a relative filling up of the older states in the east, especially those that showed little structural change toward greater industrialization and commercial activity. But perhaps some brief illustrations will help to add conviction.

It was noted by the Superintendent of the Seventh Census

that, of the northern states and in proportion to their populations, Vermont and Connecticut had contributed most to internal migration.[5] Vermont is of particular interest, because of all the states admitted to the Union by 1800 it experienced the greatest percentage fall in the refined birth ratio between then and 1860, while retaining throughout the lowest proportion of urban population.[6] It has been studied in detail by L. D. Stilwell.[7] The settlement of Vermont dates from the 1760s: "They came . . . to get new lands that were both good and cheap. The older New England hives were crowded and were sending forth new swarms."[8] At first, until the end of the eighteenth century and beginning of the nineteenth, population grew very rapidly, as a result of both immigration and a high rate of natural increase (the latter being assisted by a low age at marriage and an age distribution probably containing relatively few old people).[9] Summing up for this early period, Stilwell says:

> The conclusion of the whole matter seems to be that Vermont was prospering, but prospering within limits. Until or unless some revolution should occur in transportation or in industry, there was room for only about so many successful families. If the population increased, under the existing conditions, beyond a certain fairly immediate limit, the people on the economic margin were likely to suffer or else be forced to leave.[10]

In fact, emigration from Vermont had already begun in the late eighteenth century. There was a movement into northern New York, while in the 1790s the "Genesee fever" took others to western New York. Some went even farther to northeastern Pennsylvania and to Ohio. Stilwell admits he finds it difficult to give a full explanation of this early emigration, since prosperity was still fairly general in Vermont; then he continues:

But we do know that about three-quarters of the migra-

tion came from the four older counties of southern
Vermont, and that about three-fourths of those who
emigrated were under thirty years of age [not including
children]. If one places these facts alongside of the high
birth rate of those days, and remembers that the southern Vermont settlements were now about a generation
old, the answer seems fairly clear. The children were
growing up. Finding no room for homes of their own
on the old farm, they were moving elsewhere.[11]

After 1808, however, a series of reverses suffered by the Vermont economy put an end to immigration into the state and
turned the trickle of emigration into "a flood," "an exodus."[12]
The outward movement continued in the 1820s and 1830s,
with a new push from the introduction of sheep and large
farms, while from the 1840s there was a pull from factories
on the seaboard.[13] The rate of growth of population, already
diminishing before 1810, now fell away sharply.[14]

But even without these special factors operating after ca.
1808, Stilwell emphasises that "there would still have been
a considerable overflow attributable directly to the high birth
rate of the early days. . . . the children came and grew. And
as soon as they grew up, there was no room for them at
home or anywhere else in the vicinity. One or two of the
boys might stay on and take over the old farm. But in a
stationary or a declining economic structure, the surplus
younger generation had no alternative but emigration. It was
a clear case of the application of the laws of Malthus in their
simplest terms."[15]

In turn, the experience of Vermont seems to have been
repeated in the Genesee Valley of western New York, to
which Vermonters, together with others from Maine and
New Hampshire and (beginning rather earlier) southern New
England had migrated. In the words of N. A. McNall: "The
reasons for emigration from Vermont, which Stilwell has
summarized, hold with slight modification for Maine and

New Hampshire as well, and apply with almost equal accuracy
to the upper Genesee Valley during the decline of that area."[16]
In the early decades of the nineteenth century, the rate of
growth of population in the counties studied by McNall was
very high, but by the 1840s and 1850s there are clear signs
that the valley was filling up.[17] "In 1860 when Allegany
County included some 4,400 farms, there were 4,500 male[s]
in the county between the ages of ten and twenty, many of
whom would want farms within the next decade."[18] McNall
concludes: "Most of the gains in population in the valley in
the years between 1860 and 1950 can be explained by the
growth of Rochester to be the metropolis of the valley and
the third largest city in the state."[19]

The situation in the South may have been more complex
because of the existence of slaves and plantations: this is the
impression given by A. G. Smith in his work on the state of
South Carolina, which we take as our final example.[20] Plantations tended to displace small farmers, there was some en-
grossing of land by planters, and cotton growing was a potent
factor in soil exhaustion.[21] Migration from the state began
in the early nineteenth century, when the typical emigrant
was a small farmer; in the period 1820-60 the total outward
movement is estimated at over 200,000 white people, farmers
and planters and/or their sons and daughters, the chief attraction being more fertile land farther west.[22] Smith goes on to
say:

> Among the reasons for emigration which have been ad-
> vanced is scarcity of land in this State. South Carolina,
> it has been said, was relatively small and characterized
> by the high birth rates typical of rural areas at the time.
> As population grew, the most fertile and readily available
> lands were taken up. Unless the State could increase the
> area of improved land, it would have to give up part of
> its population, reduce birth rates, or divert resources out
> of agriculture.[23]

Even in 1860, however, there was still a large amount of
potentially cultivable land lying uncleared in South Carolina—
though much of it was "only theoretically available" and
"lack of enough readily procurable land to provide for a
planter's children often led to emigration." Smith emphasizes
that "land scarcity is a relative term" and quotes with ap-
proval L. C. Gray's statement in his *History of Agriculture
in the Southern United States to 1860* that "the scarcity of
land in older areas was not absolute, but relative to the great
abundance of fertile land available in frontier regions."[24]
(This must be conceded as true, but we can do so without
upsetting the point we are concerned to illustrate in this
chapter, which is that cheap, fertile land was much less
readily available in the older states for young people wish-
ing to marry and set up new homesteads, thus constituting
a significant impediment in comparison with more thinly
settled areas.)

While we have treated internal migration as broad evidence
of a tendency toward filling up in regions of older settlement,
or the diminishing availability of easily accessible land near
the place of residence, it is basic to Yasuba's thesis that this
movement was not without frictions. The argument can be
stated hypothetically in this way: suppose, for the purpose
of exposition, there was a customary age at which young
people expected to be able to marry, and suppose that they
would leave immediately and go to any other part of the
country if there was no opportunity to acquire a good,
cheap farm in their locality when they reached that age.
It is possible to conceive of an outflow so perfectly adjusted
that the death or retirement of older people, in conjunction
with remaining opportunities for partition of farms, might
create just enough vacancies for newly formed agricultural
households to allow the young people remaining behind to
continue marrying at the same age as before. If this were so,
and if intramarital fertility had been completely uncontrolled,

we would expect to find a tendency toward equality of standardized refined birth ratios in all states and territories— for there was always cheap land available *somewhere* during the period in question.[25] (For the moment we are assuming that population density is the only determinant of fertility to be considered; in practice, of course, differences in the degree of urbanization might also have played a part.) In effect, Yasuba's thesis rests on an assumption that although the safety valve of internal migration did operate, it was not so effective as to prevent the emergence of delays to marriage in the more fully settled areas; that those who chose to remain behind instead of migrating tended on average to defer marriage for a time, hoping perhaps to benefit later by inheritance of the home farm (just as others must have been waiting and hoping in western Europe), saving to buy higher priced land nearby, or what you will.[26] To put the matter in yet another way: it rests on an assumption that the growth of population in relation to land resources in given areas, combined with a lack of perfect mobility, led to the beginnings and gradual spread of what Hajnal has called a "European" marriage pattern characterized by a higher age of women at marriage and a higher proportion who never married at all.[27] It is possible also that incentives toward family limitation within marriage would have been affected.

Fertility Ratio, Adult-Farm Ratio, and Urban Proportion: Rank Correlation Methods

We are now to seek an alternative measure of the availability of easily accessible land in the separate states and territories at census dates between 1800 and 1860. Our main object will be to find one that can be based on data relating more directly to the period under review, instead of population density per 1,000 acres of arable land, for which Yasuba uses cropland in the year 1949.

It seemed to us that the relative potentialities of different states and territories for additional rural settlement could be measured by comparing the number of adult whites contained in each at a given time with the number of farms to be found there at some not-too-distant future time—certainly a date much earlier than 1949. The change in the numerator—from population of all ages as used by Yasuba to persons aged fifteen or sixteen and over as used by us—is not perhaps of any great consequence, though logically it seems a little more satisfactory. The change in the denominator may be more important, since it gives the measure greater contemporary relevance and takes some account also of regional farming characteristics (for example, differences between intensive and extensive agriculture). To distinguish our measure from Yasuba's population density we have called it the adult-farm ratio. A relatively low adult-farm ratio in a particular state or territory would suggest that, at the time when it applied and by comparison with other states whose adult-farm ratios were then higher, there were unusually good opportunities for the creation of additional homesteads; a relatively high adult-farm ratio might be taken as an indication that, for the area concerned, rural settlement was more nearly complete. (As we have seen, it could also reflect a high degree of urbanization. We shall return to this later.)

Farm numbers in the separate states and territories have always been changing over time; for this reason, there must be an arbitrary element in the selection of any particular census from which the denominators of adult-farm ratios are to be drawn. We have thought it desirable to compute alternative results based on farm numbers in three census years: 1850, 1860, and 1880. Of these, our selection of the last is perhaps the easiest to explain.

Results based on farm numbers in 1880 represent a compromise between two criteria of choice: first, that the data should be closely related to conditions in the period 1800-1860, so as to avoid the sort of criticism that can be made of Yasuba's use of cropland at a date as late as 1949; and second, that the relative numbers of farms in the different states should be approaching stability, so as to give a reasonably accurate impression of their respective potentials for rural settlement—an impression which would not be changed too radically if we shifted forward to consider the relative numbers of farms in different states revealed in a census ten or twenty years later.[1] The year 1880 seemed close enough to the period under review, while by that time the proportionate increases in farm numbers were tending to taper off quite sharply in the areas with which our analysis is concerned.[2] In states of the New England and Middle Atlantic divisions, farm numbers had reached a maximum by 1880 and then showed a slight tendency to decline in the period up to World War I; states of the East North Central division, which had experienced unequal increases ranging between 20 percent and 56 percent in the 1870s, dropped to a range of minus 6 percent to plus 12 percent in the 1880s. Many states still showed a solid growth of farm numbers after 1880, but the really massive proportionate increases—such as those of 243, 313, 120, 252, and 2,046 percent recorded in the 1850s for Wisconsin, Iowa, Arkansas, Texas, and California— were over. On balance, data of farms for the year 1880 seemed to represent an acceptable compromise.

There is a difficulty, however, arising from agricultural change in southern states after the Civil War. Here some of the older states, which had shown relatively small percentage increases of farm numbers in the 1850s, suddenly experienced much larger increases in the 1860s and/or 1870s. These included Maryland, the Carolinas, Georgia, Kentucky, Tennessee, Alabama, Mississippi, and Louisiana. The Superintendent of the Tenth Census of 1880 attributed the increases of farm numbers mainly to subdivision of "the great plantations of twenty and ten years ago," which had been "steadily undergoing partition, in consequence of the social and industrial changes in progress since the civil war."[3] The only way in which the influence of these changes could be excluded was to go back to a pre-Civil War year, prior to this subdivision of plantations, when farm numbers could be expected to reflect more accurately the relative potentialities of these states for rural settlement as they might have appeared to persons living in them during the period 1800-1860. Finally, we thought it worthwhile to try a third set of calculations where farm numbers are drawn from the earliest year for which they become available, that is, 1850. Here the compromise between the two criteria of choice stated at the beginning of the preceding paragraph is not so well preserved, but the objective of relating the data as closely as possible to contemporary technical conditions seems likely to be more fully achieved.

There is another way in which we have departed from Yasuba's methods. In examining the association between the adult-farm ratio of a state or territory and the white refined birth ratio we thought it desirable to introduce a ten-year time lag. For any given census, refined birth ratios (children aged zero to nine per 1,000 women aged sixteen to forty-four) depend on numbers of births during the preceding ten years, from which those still living go to make up our numerators; as a minimum lag, therefore, it seems reasonable that birth ratios should be associated with values of the factors postulated as determinants of fertility

at a date ten years earlier. Thus at the beginning of the
period, the refined birth ratio of a state or territory in 1800
is related to the adult-farm ratio calculated on the number
of adults in 1790, with a similar lag for all later census years.[4]

Results obtained by computing Kendall's coefficient of
rank correlation between the white refined birth ratio and
the adult-farm ratio in a state or territory are shown in
table 1, where the numbers of observations range from
sixteen for all states and territories at the beginning of the
period to thirty-two at the end. (Standardized refined birth
ratios are used for 1830 and later dates.)[5] In general, the inverse associations are strikingly similar to those derived by
Yasuba from his calculations based on population density
per 1,000 acres of arable land, when arable land is taken as
cropland in the year 1949 (see above, table A). When computed for all states and territories, our coefficients show a
slightly closer inverse association than Yasuba's in 1800 and
again from 1830 to 1860; like his, they are all significant at
the 1 percent level. The downward trend in the coefficient,
which for Yasuba appeared after 1810, seems now to be postponed until after 1830, emerging in cross sections for the
years 1840, 1850, and 1860.

When states and territories are divided into free and slave,
the chief differences between Yasuba's work and our own
arise from the closer inverse associations obtained for slave
states and territories; on the whole, this remains true whether
we base adult-farm ratios on farm numbers in 1850, 1860, or
1880.

To take account of the correlation between the two supposed
determinants of fertility—population density per 1,000 acres of
arable land and the proportion of urban population—Yasuba
used his method of "standardized rank correlation" or "moving standardization" (see above, p. 10). We have preferred to
compute Kendall's coefficient of partial rank correlation. If
we identify the adult-farm ratio of a state or territory as vari-

Table 1. Kendall's Coefficient of Rank Correlation (τ)
between the White Refined Birth Ratio and the
Adult-Farm Ratio in a State or Territory:
United States, 1800-1860

	1800	1810	1820	1830	1840	1850	1860
For all states and territories, with adult-farm ratios based on farm numbers in:							
1850	-.78**	-.78**	-.71**	-.83**	-.79**	-.70**	
1860	-.78**	-.82**	-.71**	-.83**	-.79**	-.70**	-.69**
1880	-.78**	-.88**	-.84**	-.88**	-.80**	-.68**	-.69**
For free states and territories, with adult-farm ratios based on farm numbers in:							
1850	-.72**	-.83**	-.75**	-.82**	-.78**	-.62**	
1860	-.72**	-.89**	-.71**	-.85**	-.84**	-.67**	-.74**
1880	-.67*	-.89**	-.82**	-.88**	-.93**	-.67**	-.73**
For slave states and territories, with adult-farm ratios based on farm numbers in:							
1850	-.90**	-.90**	-.79**	-.89**	-.76**	-.80**	
1860	-.81*	-.81*	-.71*	-.85**	-.69**	-.76**	-.77**
1880	-.90**	-.90**	-.79**	-.85**	-.65**	-.63**	-.73**

Note: Coefficients opposite the dates 1850, 1860, and 1880 in the stub column apply only to those states and territories that had approximately the same boundaries in the years for which refined birth ratios and adult-farm ratios are calculated as in the year from which farm numbers have been drawn for use in adult-farm ratios. (Standardized refined birth ratios are used for 1830 and later.)

*Significant at the 5% level.
**Significant at the 1% level.

Table 2. Kendall's Coefficient of Partial Rank Correlation $(\tau_{13.2})$
between the White Refined Birth Ratio and the Adult-Farm
Ratio in a State or Territory

| | *Adult-farm ratios based on farm numbers in:* | | | *Yasuba's coefficient of standardized rank correlation* |
	1850	*1860*	*1880*	
1800	−.76	−.75	−.76	−.825
1810	−.76	−.79	−.87	−.806
1820	−.64	−.64	−.79	−.787
1830	−.77	−.76	−.84	−.705
1840	−.73	−.73	−.76	−.371
1850	−.50	−.51	−.50	−.510
1860		−.52	−.56	−.419

Note: The proportion of urban population by state or territory used
in calculating Kendall's coefficient of partial rank correlation was
taken from U.S. Bureau of the Census, *Sixteenth Census of the United
States, 1940—Population,* vol. 1, *Number of Inhabitants* (Washington,
D.C.: 1942), pp. 20-24 (urban proportions in 1790), and Yasuba,
Birth Rates, table 5.3, pp. 143-44. Standardized refined birth ratios
are used from 1830 onward. For Yasuba's coefficient of rank correlation between the white refined birth ratio and population density,
when states and territories are standardized with respect to the proportion of urban population, see his table 5.13, p. 174.

able 1, the proportion of urban population as variable 2, and
the white refined birth ratio as variable 3, results can be set
out as in table 2. (Yasuba's coefficients of standardized rank
correlation between population density and the refined birth
ratio are included for comparison.)

At the first four dates (1800-1830), there is a fair measure
of consistency between Kendall's coefficients of partial rank
correlation calculated for our data and Yasuba's coefficients
of standardized rank correlation. All hold up well, although
Yasuba's coefficients differ in that they show a very mild
downward trend. A major difference arises in 1840, when
Yasuba's coefficient falls suddenly to about half its former
value, whereas our partial coefficients, although slightly

lower than in 1830, remain at nearly the same level. Finally, in 1850 and 1860, the earlier broad consistency between the different measures is restored.

In all cross sections, Kendall's coefficient of partial rank correlation between the refined birth ratio and the adult-farm ratio in a state or territory ($\tau_{13.2}$) is higher than that between the refined birth ratio and the proportion of urban population ($\tau_{23.1}$). If we use adult-farm ratios based on farm numbers in 1850 (first row), 1860 (second row), and 1880 (third row), coefficients of partial rank correlation between the refined birth ratio and the proportion of urban population are as follows[6] (Yasuba's coefficients of standardized rank correlation between the refined birth ratio and urban proportion have been included in brackets for comparison):

1800	1810	1820	1830	1840	1850	1860
−.30	−.17	−.22	−.17	−.04	−.37	
−.25	−.08	−.21	−.17	−.05	−.38	−.33
−.32	−.12	−.13	−.18	−.16	−.44	−.32
(−.333)	(−.250)	(−.343)	(−.214)	(−.389)	(−.391)	(−.346)

Compared with those in table 2, these results might be interpreted to give some further support to Yasuba's view that, although the influence of urbanization probably increased in the latter part of the period, "it was not until after the Civil War . . . that the relative importance of the two factors was reversed." (However, it will be suggested later that our confidence in assessing the relative importance of the two determinants may need to be qualified to some extent in the light of additional considerations to be introduced in chapter 7.)

4

Fertility Ratio, Adult-Farm Ratio, and Urban Proportion: Multiple Regression

As we have seen, neither Yasuba's coefficient of standardized rank correlation nor Kendall's coefficient of partial rank correlation can be tested for significance. We have now to seek a method that will yield results not subject to this deficiency.

Something can be done by means of an alternative treatment of the data. As an experiment, we prepared a set of scatter diagrams—one for each census date—in which the refined birth ratio of a state or territory (on the vertical axis) was plotted against the logarithm of its adult-farm ratio at a date ten years earlier. Each diagram embodied a cross section of the data at a given time, and they all suggested a roughly linear relation between the variables—a relation that would, of course, be curvilinear if plotted for the natural value of the adult-farm ratio instead of its logarithm. Sometimes there tended to be a loss of linearity at extremely low values of the logarithms of adult-farm ratios, when the scatters became convex upward;[1] but apart from upper levels of birth ratios where they had the appearance of being near a "ceiling," there was a strong impression of linearity over the rest of the range. If we think of this in terms of the natural values of adult-farm ratios instead of their logarithms, it implies, in each cross section, that given increases in the supposed explanatory variable were associated with diminishing reductions in birth ratios. Such a relation would be consistent with common sense, since there might well have been a "floor" to birth ratios as well as a ceiling and greater resistance to change in a state or territory where fertility was closer to this lower level.

Roughly linear relations were suggested also by scatter

26

diagrams in which the refined birth ratio of a state or territory at a given time was plotted against the logarithm of the proportion of urban population at a date ten years earlier, though these scatters were not nearly as tight and the associations tended to be obscured by the existence of some states and territories whose urban proportions had the common feature of being recorded as zero but which showed a range of widely different refined birth ratios—corresponding, perhaps, to differences in their adult-farm ratios.[2]

Thus in place of rank correlation methods, we were encouraged to try multiple regression analysis, based on logarithmic transformation of the two explanatory variables. For each cross section we postulated a model in which

$Y_{(t)}$ = the white refined birth ratio of a state or territory (unstandardized for the first three cross sections and standardized for 1830 and later),

$X_{1(t-10)}$ = the adult-farm ratio at a date ten years earlier, and

$X_{2(t-10)}$ = the proportion of urban population (in percentage points) at a date ten years earlier.

The regression will be

$$Y_{(t)} = a_{(t)} + \beta_1 \log X_{1(t-10)} + \beta_2 \log X_{2(t-10)} + \epsilon_{(t)},$$

where $a_{(t)}$ is a constant for all states and territories at a given time and $\epsilon_{(t)}$ is a random term assumed to be normally distributed about a mean of zero, with a constant standard deviation and not correlated with either of the two explanatory variables.

We wish to know whether the estimates of the partial regression coefficients β_1 and β_2 are significantly different from zero and to compute the coefficients of partial linear correlation.

Before proceeding, we made an arbitrary adjustment to the data. At some dates, as we have just seen, the proportion of

urban population in a state or territory (1940 urban definition) was given as zero; rather than lose these observations
in the transformation to logarithms, we substituted an arbitrary
value of 0.5 percent in each case.[3]

Three sets of results were computed, with adult-farm ratios
based alternatively on farm numbers in 1850, 1860, and 1880.
In each case, and for every census date, β_1 was significantly
different from zero at the 1 percent level, but β_2 was never
significant even at the 5 percent level. The closest approach
of β_2 to significance was in the regression for the birth ratios
of 1850 when, with X_1 based on farm numbers in 1880, it
became significant at the 10 percent level (falling just short
of the 5 percent level); and in the regression for the birth
ratios of 1860 when, with X_1 based on farm numbers in
1860, it reached the 10 percent level. The results are given
in table 3.

Coefficients of partial linear correlation between the refined birth ratio of a state or territory and the logarithm of
the adult-farm ratio, and between the refined birth ratio and
the logarithm of the proportion of urban population, are
shown in table 4. For each cross section, we have also included the square of the coefficient of multiple correlation
and, for comparison, the square of the coefficient of linear
correlation derived from a simple regression of the refined
birth ratio on the logarithm of the adult-farm ratio. It will
be seen that the additional variation "explained" by the
multiple regression is usually of the order of 1 or 2 percentage
points—at its greatest, 3.7 percentage points in 1850, when
adult-farm ratios are based on farm numbers in 1880. These
are very small improvements on the variation explained by
the simple regression.

If our object is to explain interstate differences in fertility,
the adult-farm ratio has the appearance of being much more
promising as an explanatory variable than the proportion of
urban population. Refined birth ratios tended to be higher

Table 3. Parameters of Multiple Regressions of the White Refined Birth Ratio of a State or Territory on the Adult-Farm Ratio and the Proportion of Urban Population: United States, 1800–1860

	a Adult-farm ratios based on farm numbers in:			β_1 Adult-farm ratios based on farm numbers in:			β_2 Adult-farm ratios based on farm numbers in:		
	1850	1860	1880	1850	1860	1880	1850	1860	1880
1800	2046	2003	1902	-595**	-575**	-517**	-72	-61	-57
1810	2133	2093	1945	-737**	-743**	-647**	-68	-57	-43
1820	1970	1934	1835	-506**	-499**	-515**	-104	-96	-59
1830	2125	2025	1849	-897**	-792**	-697**	-43	-64	-71
1840	2193	2008	1799	-984**	-769**	-642**	-44	-67	-63
1850	2273	1974	1716	-1103**	-761**	-536**	-92	-137	-150
1860		2024	1681		-773**	-558**		-123	-82

Note: The regression postulated is $Y_{(t)} = a_{(t)} + \beta_1 \log X_{1(t-10)} + \beta_2 \log X_{2(t-10)} + \epsilon_{(t)}$, where $Y_{(t)}$ is the white refined birth ratio of a state or territory (standardized for 1830 and later); $a_{(t)}$ is a constant for all states and territories at a given time; $X_{1(t-10)}$ is the adult-farm ratio at a date ten years earlier; and $X_{2(t-10)}$ is the proportion of urban population (in percentage points) at a date ten years earlier.

*Significant at the 5% level.
**Significant at the 1% level.

Table 4. Coefficients of Partial Linear Correlation between the White Refined Birth Ratio of a State or Territory and the Logarithms of the Adult-Farm Ratio and the Proportion of Urban Population

	Adult-farm ratio $(r_y, \log x_1 . \log x_2)$			Proportion of urban population $(r_y, \log x_2 . \log x_1)$			Square of coefficient of multiple correlation			Square of coefficient of linear correlation (Simple regression)		
	(a)	(b)	(c)	(a)	(b)	(c)	(a)	(b)	(c)	(a)	(b)	(c)
1800	-.90**	-.90**	-.94**	-.34	-.30	-.33	.859	.867	.908	.841	.854	.897
1810	-.90**	-.92**	-.97**	-.36	-.34	-.39	.865	.892	.956	.844	.878	.948
1820	-.74**	-.76**	-.86**	-.29	-.27	-.21	.700	.716	.828	.673	.693	.819
1830	-.80**	-.81**	-.89**	-.10	-.16	-.24	.795	.797	.884	.793	.792	.877
1840	-.80**	-.77**	-.84**	-.11	-.16	-.18	.767	.739	.810	.764	.732	.804
1850	-.66**	-.65**	-.71**	-.20	-.31	-.38	.752	.745	.779	.742	.719	.742
1860		-.70**	-.77**		-.30	-.23		.773	.795		.750	.784

Note: (a) Adult-farm ratios based on farm numbers in 1850; (b) adult-farm ratios based on farm numbers in 1860; (c) adult-farm ratios based on farm numbers in 1880. Deletion of the observations of the birth ratios of Kentucky and Tennessee in 1800, Indiana in 1820, and Illinois in 1830 (see note 1 to this chapter) would have the effect of reducing the partial correlation coefficients between adult-farm ratios and refined birth ratios in 1800 and raising them in 1820 and 1830. In 1800 they would become -.81**, -.83**, and -.89**; in 1820, -.84**, -.86**, and -.94**; in 1830, -.85**, -.86**, and -.92**. The partial correlation coefficients between urban proportions and refined birth ratios would also be affected. In 1800 they would become -.33, -.29, and -.34; in 1820, -.19, -.17, and -.15; in 1830, +.01, -.04, and -.23.

The square of the coefficient of linear correlation is derived from a simple regression of the white refined birth ratio on the logarithm of the adult-farm ratio.

*Significant at the 5% level.
**Significant at the 1% level.

in more thinly settled areas, where adult-farm ratios were
lower and, presumably, economic opportunities in agriculture were more abundant—this after we have taken account
of differences in levels of urbanization. It would seem that
this generalization could be applied to cross sections at all
census dates in the period 1800-1860, since even toward
its end, the adult-farm ratio continues to dominate the
multiple regressions. Possibly there was a slight strengthen-
ing of the influence of urban proportions near the mid-
century, but even here the signs are not clear cut on the
evidence so far. Broadly, results are consistent with those
obtained by rank correlation methods, though the analysis
in this section has the advantage of allowing us to apply
tests of significance to the partial coefficients which it
yields.

It is convenient at this point to draw attention to a difficulty
relating to the interpretation of our analysis. We have treated
adult-farm ratios as broad indicators of relative economic
opportunities in agriculture in different states and territories—
the lower the adult-farm ratio, the greater the opportunities,
unexploited so far, for the establishment of new rural households—and these in turn are assumed to have been factors
helping to explain interstate differences of fertility. It is
possible, however, to think of the relation as operating in
an opposite direction, so that high birth ratios are seen as
determinants of relatively low adult-farm ratios, and low
birth ratios are seen as determinants of high adult-farm ratios.
This can be illustrated in the following hypothetical example.

Suppose there are two purely agricultural communities, A
and B, which we are examining by cross-section analysis. At
the date to which the investigation relates, they have equal
populations of adults, and both have very large supplies of
unused land. In the course of time, there is no movement into or out of either area. For some reason (not connected with
economic opportunities in agriculture), A has a higher refined

birth ratio than B. Other things being equal, A's population
will grow faster than B's, and at the future date on which
we count farm numbers in the two areas for use in calculating adult-farm ratios, A will have a larger population and
hence more farms than B. If so, A's adult-farm ratio as
measured at the initial date will be lower than B's, since
their populations are taken then to have been equal, but
the number of farms forming the denominator of the ratio
in A's case will be greater than in B's. We might be tempted
to assume that the lower adult-farm ratio in A explains its
higher birth ratio, whereas in this illustration it is the higher
birth ratio in A that explains its lower adult-farm ratio as
measured at the earlier time.

There may well be an element of this kind in our analysis,
but we think it most unlikely to have been important as a
factor giving rise to the high partial correlations we have obtained between the refined birth ratio of a state or territory
and the adult-farm ratio—though it may possibly have strengthened them to some slight extent. We feel this for two main
reasons. First, there is the fact of movement across state
borders in response to the attraction of cheap land. This
played a considerable role in determining the relative rates
of population growth in different states and territories, re-
inforcing and perhaps outweighing the effects of differences
in their refined birth ratios. Migration would tend to reduce
the importance of the reverse relation which affected initial
levels of adult-farm ratios in our imaginary illustration, even
if in all other respects the illustration truly reflected reality.
Second, we chose the date 1880 as one of our bases for the
calculation of adult-farm ratios partly with this problem in
mind. By that time, as we have seen, the outlines of settlement in the states and territories included in our analysis
were tending to harden. There was still room for change, but
relative farm numbers in 1880 do not seem likely to mis-
represent too grossly the ultimate economic opportunities

offered for agricultural settlement in the various areas concerned—"ultimate" being understood, of course, in the context of a technological environment not far removed from that of the period 1800-1860. Innovation and institutional change make the problem of defining relative economic opportunities in agriculture similar to that encountered by a kitten chasing its own tail: inevitably the target keeps moving. But the broad consistency of results based on different years—1850, 1860, 1880, and (in Yasuba's work) 1949—makes us feel that the inverse associations between birth ratios and adult-farm ratios (or "population density") contain real meaning and that relative economic opportunities in agriculture may well have been a major determinant of interstate differences in levels of fertility. After all, this is a perfectly reasonable view a priori, and one that finds a parallel in recent work on the historical demography of some parts of northwestern Europe, where it is thought birth rates tended to be higher in more thinly settled regions.[4] Nevertheless, the very strength of the coefficients of partial correlation between the refined birth ratio of a state or territory and the adult-farm ratio requires that they be subjected to further interrogation, since the associations they indicate are often closer than we should expect to find when dealing with socioeconomic variables, however persuasive the theory suggesting the likely existence of a relation between them. This examination will be undertaken in chapter 7.

5

Rural Fertility Ratio and Economic Opportunity in Agriculture

We suggested earlier that there may be a further source of uncertainty affecting Yasuba's analysis, connected with his treatment of urbanization. (It could also affect our own work, in what has been done so far.) Our object in this chapter will be to discuss the nature of this difficulty and to ask how it could be surmounted.

It will be remembered that the aim of Yasuba's cross-section analysis was to study separately the relation between the refined birth ratio of a state or territory and each of the socioeconomic variables postulated as determinants of fertility. To do this, he had to take account of what we have called the cross-correlation between "population density" (per 1,000 acres of arable land) and the proportion of urban population (see above pp. 9-10). By his method of "standardized rank correlation" he measured the associations between birth ratios and population densities, when states and territories were standardized with respect to urban proportions; and similarly, when dealing with the associations between birth ratios and urban proportions, he hoped to eliminate the influence of differences in population densities. We have followed a similar path. After substituting adult-farm ratios for Yasuba's population densities, we calculated coefficients of partial rank correlation, the latter being a measure that, in principle, is not unlike his "standardized rank correlation." Again, our multiple regression analysis was intended to test, in successive cross sections, the relation between the refined birth ratio and each of the two variables after eliminating the influence of the other.

A point coming to mind, however, is that in analyses of this kind we may have to consider not only the number of urban inhabitants in a state or territory (in proportion to its total population) but also the nature of their distribution between towns and cities of different sizes. In effect, when standardizing with respect to urban proportions, Yasuba gives equal weight to any urban inhabitant, whatever the size of the place in which that person lived; and in computing coefficients of partial correlation (rank or linear), we have done the same. This would not matter if there turned out to be no relation between the urban refined birth ratio and town or city size; and even if there were, other characteristics of the data might render it innocuous from the point of view of statistical analysis of the kind just described. This would be so, for example, if the distribution of urban inhabitants between large, middle-sized, and small towns did not differ significantly from one state or territory to another. But we know the latter condition is unlikely to have been satisfied; and on grounds of general reasoning, it would not be surprising if urban fertility tended to be lower, the larger the size of place. (Urban refined birth ratios might also have been affected by differences in the mortality of children relative to that of adult women. Possibly this would have been higher in large towns.) We decided to look more closely at the statistics for one census year to see what pattern of urban birth ratios emerges.

Here we chose the Sixth Census of 1840, the last in the period 1800-1860 which reported age distributions for units as small as townships. Even here the *Compendium* lists age distributions only for "principal towns," although these include nearly all of the places falling within the U.S. Bureau of the Census 1940 urban definition (126 out of a total of 131).[1] For these we calculated white refined birth ratios (number of children aged zero to nine per 1,000 women aged sixteen to forty-four)[2] and standardized them indirectly by Yasuba's method to the age distribution of women within the childbearing span in 1860.[3] Our purpose was to prepare

scatter diagrams relating the standardized white refined birth
ratio of an urban place to the size of its population (white
and nonwhite). Since the number of observations for a state
was often quite small, some degree of aggregation was necessary; but if carried too far, this would have thrown together
observations for areas between which refined birth ratios
(calculated for total populations, both urban and rural) were
fairly widely different. After some experiment, we decided
to use a separate scatter diagram for each census division,
though even here a paucity of observations in the West North
Central and West South Central divisions led us to combine
each one with its East Central counterpart.

When plotted, the scatters proved to be very loose, although
there was some suggestion of a weak inverse association between the urban standardized white refined birth ratio and
size of place. We have not thought it worthwhile to reproduce
the diagrams here, but it may be of some interest to set out
the coefficients of linear correlation, which run as follows:[4]

New England	−.26
Middle Atlantic	−.38
South Atlantic	−.22
North Central (East and West)	−.50
South Central (East and West)	−.18

The coefficients for the Middle Atlantic division and North
Central (East and West) are significant at the 5 percent level,
while that for New England is significant at the 10 percent
level. The other two are not significant, even at 10 percent.

Percentage distributions of urban population, by size of
place, for states and territories have been shown in table 5.
Clearly there were wide differences: even if we limit our inspection to the three most highly urbanized states (Rhode
Island, Massachusetts, and Louisiana), we find 97 percent
of Louisiana's urban population in New Orleans, a large town
of 102,193 inhabitants, while the most urbanized state of all,
Rhode Island, had no place of more than 25,000. Massachu-

setts occupied an intermediate position, with one-third of its urban population in Boston, which then had 93,383 inhabitants.

It would be difficult to say how far we should allow considerations of this kind to affect our confidence in results presented earlier in this work. Perhaps, with the exercise of sufficient ingenuity, the urban proportion of a state or territory used in partial analysis could be "weighted" in some way to take account of the distribution of urban inhabitants by size of place, but inevitably such a procedure would introduce arbitrary elements likely to open up fresh doubts. A much more straightforward check on the relation between the refined birth ratio and relative economic opportunity in agriculture can be made by a change of method that leaves aside techniques of multiple regression or partial correlation. This alternative method calls for considerable labor in assembling the necessary data but, once this has been done, allows us to proceed immediately by simple rank correlation.

For censuses of the period 1800-1840, we have subtracted the urban components (U.S. Bureau of the Census 1940 definition) of total numbers in the relevant age groups recorded for a state or territory and so calculated *rural* white refined birth ratios.[5] In 1830 and 1840, when the age classification improves, these were standardized indirectly to the age distribution of women within the childbearing span in 1860. Results are shown in table 6.

Next we calculated adult-farm ratios, in this case with numerators consisting of rural adults only, and measured their associations with rural white refined birth ratios by means of Kendall's coefficient of rank correlation.[6] These are given in table 7. (Our practice so far has been to relate the birth ratio of a state or territory at a given date to an adult-farm ratio derived from numbers of adults at a date ten years earlier. However, with the available data, it was sometimes difficult to trace the populations of townships

Table 5. Distribution of Urban Population, by Size of Place, for States and
Territories: United States, 1840 (U.S. Bureau of
the Census 1940 urban-rural definition)

Size of place	2,500–5,000	5,000–10,000	10,000–25,000	25,000–50,000	50,000–100,000	100,000–250,000	250,000–500,000	Total
	%	%	%	%	%	%	%	%
New England								
Maine	-	61.3	38.7	-	-	-	-	100.0
New Hampshire	28.5	71.5	-	-	-	-	-	100.0
Vermont	-	-	-	-	-	-	-	-
Massachusetts	6.5	34.9	25.2	-	33.4	-	-	100.0
Rhode Island	8.8	42.6	48.6	-	-	-	-	100.0
Connecticut	28.2	38.5	33.3	-	-	-	-	100.0
Middle Atlantic								
New York	-	3.8	15.0	14.8	-	-	66.4	100.0
New Jersey	37.1	19.2	43.7	-	-	-	-	100.0
Pennsylvania	10.9	7.4	22.1	29.2	30.4	-	-	100.0
South Atlantic								
Delaware	-	100.0	-	-	-	-	-	100.0
Maryland	5.6	4.6	-	-	-	89.8	-	100.0
District of Columbia	-	40.3	59.7	-	-	-	-	100.0
Virginia	10.5	29.5	60.0	-	-	-	-	100.0
North Carolina	59.9	40.1	-	-	-	-	-	100.0
South Carolina	12.9	-	-	87.1	-	-	-	100.0
Georgia	28.5	26.0	45.5	-	-	-	-	100.0
Florida	-	-	-	-	-	-	-	-

Table 5 (cont.)

East North Central						
Ohio	22.7	21.8	-	55.5	-	100.0
Indiana	100.0	-	-	-	-	100.0
Illinois	100.0	-	-	-	-	100.0
Michigan	-	100.0	-	-	-	100.0
Wisconsin	-	-	-	-	-	-
East South Central						
Kentucky	8.9	22.6	68.5	-	-	100.0
Tennessee	-	100.0	-	-	-	100.0
Alabama	-	-	100.0	-	-	100.0
Mississippi	100.0	-	-	-	-	100.0
West North Central						
Iowa	-	-	-	-	-	-
Missouri	-	-	100.0	-	-	100.0
West South Central						
Arkansas	-	-	-	-	97.0	-
Louisiana	3.0	-	-	-	-	100.0

Source: Calculated from data of the populations of urban places, by state or territory, kindly supplied by the Population Division, U.S. Bureau of the Census.

Table 6. Rural White Refined Birth Ratio, by State or
Territory: United States, 1800-1840

	1800	*1810*	*1820*	*1830*	*1840*
New England					
Maine	1,998	1,905	1,638	1,521	1,489
New Hampshire	1,702	1,559	1,389	1,231	1,164
Vermont	2,068	1,788	1,468	1,357	1,287
Massachusetts	1,539	1,470	1,310	1,148	1,071
Rhode Island	1,569	1,505	1,398	1,165	1,130
Connecticut	1,522	1,451	1,296	1,143	1,047
Middle Atlantic					
New York	1,993	1,986	1,739	1,582	1,402
New Jersey	1,822	1,747	1,637	1,524	1,427
Pennsylvania	1,964	1,921	1,815	1,722	1,720
South Atlantic					
Delaware	1,509	1,687	1,596	1,436	1,415
Maryland	1,664	1,643	1,586	1,437	1,416
Virginia	1,840	1,795	1,726	1,675	1,633
North Carolina	1,920	1,857	1,839	1,725	1,667
South Carolina	2,089	1,987	1,888	1,817	1,757
Georgia	2,154	2,127	2,051	2,103	2,109
Florida				1,960	1,745
East North Central					
Ohio	2,500	2,306	2,145	2,011	1,818
Indiana	2,014	2,307	2,235	2,237	2,016
Illinois		2,201	2,235	2,275	1,944
Michigan		2,121	1,826	1,860	1,623
Wisconsin					1,517
East South Central					
Kentucky	2,371	2,276	2,086	2,043	1,936
Tennessee	2,424	2,302	2,204	2,195	2,026
Alabama			2,252	2,319	2,224
Mississippi	2,509	2,089	2,222	2,254	2,139
West North Central					
Iowa					1,874
Missouri			2,189	2,370	2,350

Table 6 (*cont.*)

	1800	1810	1820	1830	1840
West South Central					
Arkansas			2,159	2,273	2,259
Louisiana		2,202	1,978	1,940	1,946

Note: Urban components of state populations have been removed according to the U.S. Bureau of the Census 1940 urban-rural definition (see note 5 to this chapter). The white refined birth ratio is the number of children aged 0-9 per 1,000 women aged 16-44. Standardized ratios are given for 1830 and 1840; the method of standardization is that described by Yasuba, *Birth Rates*, pp. 128-30, and table 4.12, pp. 131-32, note *a*.

Source: For a state or territory not containing an urban place, Yasuba, *Birth Rates*, tables 2.7 and 4.12, pp. 61-62 and 131-32; otherwise calculated from U.S. censuses.

Table 7. Kendall's Coefficient of Rank Correlation (τ) between the Rural White Refined Birth Ratio and the Adult-Farm Ratio in a State or Territory: United States, 1800-1840

	Adult-farm ratios based on farm numbers in:	
	1860†	*1880†*
1800	-.72**	-.70**
1810	-.82**	-.78**
1820	-.72**	-.84**
1830	-.80**	-.82**
1840	-.75**	-.69**

Note: Numerators of adult-farm ratios comprise rural adults only.

*Significant at the 5% level.
**Significant at the 1% level.
†Only those states and territories included in calculations for the corresponding rows of table 1 and columns of table 2.

back to an earlier census; therefore the variables now being correlated have not been separated by a ten-year interval.)

There is a strong inverse association at each of the five census dates, and they are all significant at the 1 percent level. Thus the data are not inconsistent with the postulate that relative levels of rural fertility in the different states and territories depended on the ease or difficulty of establishing new rural households. And since we are dealing with a predominantly rural society, this factor can be expected to have been reflected in statewide fertility levels; that is, in differentials of the refined birth ratio as measured for all white women of childbearing age, both urban and rural.

Rural Fertility Ratio and Intrastate Differences in Densities of Settlement

Although it was not practicable for Yasuba to use units smaller than states and territories, he emphasizes that "an index of the availability of land for an area as large and variable in size as the state is bound to be crude" (p. 160). We decided to look in more detail at two states in which, for a time, there tended to be barriers that led to a greater concentration of settlement in a part of the state area. These are Virginia and New York. For some time after the easing of obstacles to the spread of land occupation, each could be expected to include an older, more densely settled portion and a newer, more lightly settled one. We wish to measure these intrastate differences in densities of settlement and to know whether they were associated with corresponding differences in white refined birth ratios. As in the preceding chapter, analysis will be confined to rural birth ratios, while rural adults only will be included in the numerators of adult-farm ratios (1940 urban-rural definition).

For various reasons, settlement was confined mainly to eastern Virginia and southeastern New York until the War of Independence, after which population flowed out to settle the rest of these states. The contrast is seen easily in Virginia; there, in 1863, the new state of West Virginia was formed largely from counties lying over the Allegheny Mountains, an area in which settlement had not begun until the 1790s. For the period 1800-1860 and in accordance with the later division, we have grouped the counties of Virginia, as it then stood, into eastern and western areas and calculated separate rural adult-farm ratios and rural white refined birth ratios,[1] as shown in table 8.

As we should expect, adult-farm ratios (calculated for rural

Table 8. Virginia: Adult-Farm Ratio and Rural White Refined
Birth Ratio, Eastern and Western Areas, 1800-1860

Year	Adult-farm ratio				Rural white refined birth ratio	
	Eastern area based on farm numbers in:		Western area based on farm numbers in:		Eastern area	Western area
	1860	1880	1860	1880		
					(Unstandardized)	
1800	3.5	1.8	1.1	0.5	1,791	2,188
1810	3.7	1.9	1.4	0.7	1,725	2,168
1820	3.9	2.0	1.9	0.9	1,670	2,017
					(Standardized)	
1830	4.6	2.4	2.6	1.3	1,599	1,968
1840	4.5	2.4	3.4	1.6	1,547	1,886
1850	5.2	2.7	5.0	2.4	1,403	1,733
1860		3.4		2.7	1,416	1,659

Note: The numerator of the adult-farm ratio comprises rural adults
only (U.S. Bureau of the Census 1940 urban-rural definition). The
rural white refined birth ratio is the number of children aged 0-9 per
1,000 women aged 16-44.
Source: Calculated from U.S. censuses.

adults) were lower in the more recently settled western area,
although the proportionate difference between the two parts
narrows progressively over time. Rural white refined birth
ratios in the western area exceeded those in the east by about
21 to 26 percent during the period 1800-1850, with a smaller
difference of 17 percent emerging in 1860. Broadly, the pattern
accords with the hypothesis that fertility would tend to be
higher in areas where land was more readily available for the
creation of new rural households, though it is perhaps a little
surprising that the gap between the standardized birth ratios
did not begin to diminish earlier than appears in our estimates.
Given the marked rise of the adult-farm ratio in the western
area, relative to that in the east, we might have predicted a
priori that the downward trend of the western birth ratio

would have been more pronounced than appears in table 7. (Questions relating to the determinants of trends *over time* in white refined birth ratios, as distinguished from geographical differences at a given time, will be discussed in a more general context in chapter 7.)

For the state of New York, we have tried to deal more intensively with geographic differences of fertility as revealed in the Fourth and Fifth Censuses of 1820 and 1830. Contrasts between the white refined birth ratios of the separate counties in 1820 are shown here in figure 2.[2] (In this, the urban components of county populations have not been excluded.) This suggests a general pattern by which the lower birth ratios tend to be in the southeast, stretching westward to some extent across the central part of the state; the higher ratios tend to be in the north and more particularly the west. In fact, the gradation of birth ratios strikingly suggests the historic course of land occupation: settlement had moved slowly from the southeast corner up the Hudson River, so that by the 1770s the area around Albany was the frontier; after the War of Independence, occupation of the rest of the state went ahead rapidly.

Before calculating the coefficient of rank correlation, in 1820, between the rural white refined birth ratio and the (rural) adult-farm ratio in a county, we made several adjustments to the data. First, there were problems arising from the creation of new counties between 1820 and 1880 (the latter being the date we intended to use for the denominators of adult-farm ratios). Where a new county was formed by subdividing an existing one, it was easy enough to add together the numbers of farms in the two areas in 1880 so as to obtain a denominator for the adult-farm ratio of the original county in 1820. However, there were some cases in which a new county was constructed by putting together areas of land formerly contained in two or more others. To deal with these we found it necessary to treat as a single unit a fairly large

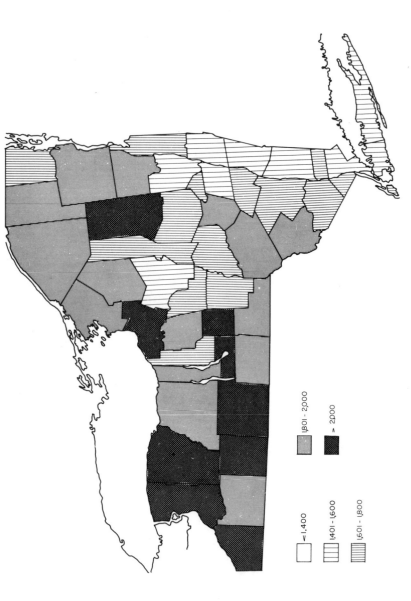

Figure 2. White refined birth ratio, by county, in the state of New York, 1820 (children aged 0–9 per 1,000 women aged 16–44).

Source: Calculated from U.S. Bureau of the Census, *Fourth Census (1820)*, bk. 1.

Legend:

- < 1,400
- 1,401 – 1,600
- 1,601 – 1,800
- 1,801 – 2,000
- > 2,000

western area comprising three counties in 1820 (Genesee, Ontario, and Seneca), which had been reorganized into nine counties by 1880. The counties of Steuben, Tioga, and Tompkins had to be omitted in 1820, together with a roughly equivalent area in 1880. These adjustments left us with a total of forty-five observations.

Next, since we wished to measure the association between rural white refined birth ratios and adult-farm ratios in which rural adults comprised the numerators, steps were taken to subtract the urban components of county totals. We dropped the city and county of New York (now leaving a total of forty-four observations) and calculated rural birth ratios for counties containing the townships of Albany, Hudson, Schenectady, Troy, and Utica, which qualify as urban places under the U.S. Bureau of the Census 1940 definition.

Kendall's coefficient of rank correlation shows a fairly close inverse association of -.67, which is significant well within the 1 percent level.[3] From this it would appear that the relationship between rural fertility and the availability of easily accessible land holds even for areas smaller than states and territories, or the broad subdivisions of a state, taken as units elsewhere in our work.[4]

Naturally, we were interested to know to what extent this result had been affected by intercounty differences in the age distribution of women within the childbearing span, which might have been more favorable to relatively high refined birth ratios in areas of recent settlement within the state. For this reason, we repeated the analysis for the census of 1830 but now with the rural white refined birth ratios standardized indirectly to the distribution of women over the childbearing ages in 1860.[5] An adjustment was also made to exclude the townships of Buffalo and Rochester, which were added to the state's urban places in 1830. Kendall's coefficient of rank correlation between the rural standardized refined birth ratio of a county and the (rural) adult-farm ratio (again based on farm numbers in 1880) was only a little lower than that for the unstandardized birth ratios of 1820, being –.64 and significant at the 1 percent level. This makes it appear that the impression of higher age-specific fertility in counties where there remained greater opportunities for additional rural settlement is not mistaken. It would be desirable, of course, to make similar calculations for other states, but there is a limit to the work that can be undertaken here.

Analytical Problems Arising from
Internal Migration

So far, we have found close inverse associations between densities of agricultural settlement (as expressed in adult-farm
ratios) and refined birth ratios. These have appeared both in
cross-section analyses that apply to the total white populations of states and territories but which take account of
differences in levels of urbanization and in those relating
solely to the rural components of state populations. A
similar inverse association has just been found *within* the
state of New York, when counties were used as units. Thus
we may be encouraged to accept the hypothesis that the
abundance or scarcity of easily accessible land in a particular
area was an important determinant of fertility via its effect
on the proportions of women ever married, their average
age at first marriage, and incentives to limit family size within marriage itself. However, as we have already noted, these
associations are frequently closer than we should expect to
find when dealing with relations between socioeconomic
variables (see above, p. 33). It all seems to fall into place too
neatly. Our purpose in this chapter, therefore, will be to
look for some other factor which could have strengthened
the relationship (as measured) between density of agricultural
settlement and the refined birth ratio and then to trace its
implications.

We believe this factor might be found in an element of selection—readily understandable, even if incapable of easy
measurement—affecting the process of internal migration.
It is possible that among the adult women who moved between states, high proportions were already married prior to
departure. If so, they may well have contributed significantly
to raise the numbers of married women among all women
aged sixteen to forty-four in the newer areas toward which

internal migration was directed. Particularly this effect
might have been felt in early years when those places were
almost empty and intakes from elsewhere were large in
comparison with the small populations of existing settlers
to whom they were added.

As we have said, this cannot be measured, but it seems to
be suggested by Yasuba's statistics of the proportion of
married women among all women aged sixteen to forty-four,
given for counties of the state of New York in 1825 and 1845
from the state censuses of those years (*Birth Rates,* pp. 188-
89). In 1825 these proportions varied greatly: from 75-78
percent in Cattaraugus, Chautauqua, and Orleans in the west
to 52-54 percent in Oneida, Washington, Dutchess, Westchester, Columbia, and New York.[1] Intuitively, we feel differences of this order are probably too large to be explained
solely by reference to the relative strength or weakness of
economic constraints upon marriage affecting those already
resident in the areas concerned. In counties where young
people growing up and approaching marriageable age enjoyed
an abundance of available land, thus experiencing few im-
pediments to early marriage, it seems likely that proportions
of married women among all women aged sixteen to forty-
four were further inflated as a result of new entry from outside. And so with states and territories.

Again, Stilwell has given a vivid impression of the importance
of wives among adult women migrating from Vermont to western New York and Ohio. "One sees the young men starting
out, frequently on foot, for the long hike to the country be-
yond the Genesee. There they selected lands, began a clearing,
and erected enough of a cabin to keep out the weather. Then
back again on foot to Vermont to get their families. Sometimes the second journey was preceded by a wedding in the
home town, and going west served as a honeymoon." And of
migration into Ohio: "There is the same preliminary migration
of young men who walk the whole distance and return the

next year to Vermont to bring out their brides."[2] (If the
wives were young, as Stilwell seems to suggest, this would
be sufficiently taken into account from 1830 onward by
standardization for differences in the age distribution of
women within the childbearing span. The important question is whether very high proportions of women aged sixteen to forty-four were already married on arrival in newly
settled areas, because single women tended not to migrate
except perhaps as grown-up daughters of older migrant
couples or as spinsters associated in some way with a migrant family.)

   If our object, simply, had been to explain interstate fertility differentials at given times and not the downward trend
of national fertility over time (which was the question with
which we began), considerations such as these could be fitted
easily enough into our interpretation of the results of cross-
section analysis. Presumably an abundance of good, unoccupied land in a state or territory, appearing to us in the
form of a relatively low adult-farm ratio, would have been
an attraction to people moving in from older-settled areas
where adult-farm ratios were higher; and if most of the women
aged sixteen to forty-four among the newcomers typically
were wives accompanying their husbands, this would have
tended to reinforce the high age-specific fertility ratios likely to be found among the settlers already established there.
Perhaps it was this factor that helped to strengthen the inverse associations we have measured between adult-farm
ratios and white refined birth ratios (after allowing, in one
way or another, for urban components of state populations)
and thus contributed to the emergence of correlation coefficients which err on the side of being suspiciously high.
But even when this is recognized, results are still consistent
with the hypothesis that interstate differences in birth ratios
can be explained by the relative abundance or scarcity of
"easily accessible land," either because of its influence on

the marriage decisions and family-building behavior of those
born and growing to maturity in the one place or because
of its influence on the pattern of internal migration. Moreover, it may well have been that the average age at first
marriage of many of those who migrated soon afterward
was affected by the *prospect* of moving to a new area where
it would be easy to establish a new agricultural household.

Greater difficulties arise, however, if we wish to use the
results of cross-section analysis to test hypotheses relating
to the causes of the downward trend *over time* of the national
white refined birth ratio. This point can best be illustrated by
imagining a strong and greatly oversimplified case.

Suppose we are dealing with a country which contains only
two states, called Vermont and Genesee. These stand at opposite extremes in terms of agricultural settlement. In Vermont, all land has been occupied, and farm numbers have
reached a maximum. (By hypothesis, we exclude subdivision
of existing farms, and there is no structural change away
from agriculture.) Genesee is empty and awaiting settlement.

We assume that in Vermont all girls are accustomed to
marry immediately on reaching a given age. For this to continue, now that Vermont has "filled up," it follows that in
any year the number of farms becoming available by the
death or retirement of their occupiers *plus* the number of
girls marrying and migrating to Genesee must equal the number of girls arriving at the customary age of marriage. (This
will be necessary if subdivision is excluded and we retain a
one-family, one-farm model.) But there are likely to be frictions in the process of internal migration, so that although
many more enterprising young people marry and move to
Genesee, not enough do so, and the equation we have just
stated does not hold. In Vermont, some marriages must be
delayed and the refined birth ratio begins to fall. The average
age of women at first marriage is rising; and moreover, there
are now greater incentives toward family limitation, since it

can be foreseen that it will be more difficult to establish sons on farms of their own. The decline in Vermont's refined birth ratio is attributable to the fullness of settlement combined with an insufficiency of out-migration. (In practice, of course, we should expect the birth ratio to begin to fall at an earlier stage, when the state was not completely filled up but cultivation was extending progressively onto its marginal lands—we can think of them as the "rock-strewn hillsides" of which R. A. Billington speaks—and prices of its intramarginal land were being forced up.)[3]

In Genesee, population grows very rapidly, both by the inflow of new settlers and by a high rate of natural increase. But it is empty at the beginning, and economic pressures associated with a scarcity of available land could hardly be expected to affect fertility for some time to come. Yet its rural white refined birth ratio, which initially is very high, begins to fall quite soon, perhaps after an interval of only one or two decades (see table 6, above). (It will be easier to think of birth ratios as having been standardized for differences in the age distribution of women within the childbearing span.) This early decline of fertility in Genesee might be ascribed to more purely demographic factors. At first it had contained an extremely high proportion of married women among all women aged sixteen to forty-four because those entering from Vermont, typically, had been wives (most of whom, probably, were not yet old enough to have daughters over fifteen). But in time, annual intakes of women aged sixteen to forty-four from Vermont tend to become smaller in proportion to the numbers of young women entering that age group from among Genesee's resident population; therefore, the proportion of married women among all women aged sixteen to forty-four declines and with it the refined birth ratio.

In time, however, Genesee begins to fill up, and its situation becomes more and more like that of Vermont. Thus its rural

standardized refined birth ratio does not tend to become
stabilized at a level lower than that obtaining at the beginning; on the contrary, it goes on falling, the latter part of
its fall being attributable to the diminishing availability of
easily accessible land. A change in its birth ratio traceable
initially to a decline in the relative importance of newly
arrived married women as a component of its population
merges, imperceptibly perhaps, into another depending more
exclusively on economic factors—in Yasuba's words, "the
degree of difficulty of obtaining new land not far from the
place of residence."

This reconstruction of what might have happened is consistent with reason and with the results we have derived so
far by cross-section analysis, including the rather surprising
strength of the partial correlations between adult-farm ratios
and refined birth ratios (which is particularly noticeable in
the earlier part of the period 1800-1860). It suggests, however, that if we wish to test hypotheses relating to the determinants of *national* trends in fertility, we should con-
centrate our cross-section analyses on the older-settled states.
Differences between the birth ratios of recently settled areas
might reflect only the varying influence of admixtures of
newcomers among whom, as we have suggested, very high
proportions of the women aged sixteen to forty-four may
already have been married before arrival. Moreover, even if
it could be shown that in recently settled states and territories
there was an association between the extent of the *increase*
over time in the adult-farm ratio and the *decrease* in the refined birth ratio,[4] the apparent relationship between the two
might be spurious and attributable simply to a third factor:
the growth of population in the areas concerned. This would
raise the adult-farm ratio and, most probably in the early
decades following immediately after the first influx of settlement, would tend to reduce the importance of annual inflows
of women aged sixteen to forty-four in comparison with the

numbers of young residents entering that age group as a simple result of growing older.

On this interpretation, the basic cause of the downward trend of the national white refined birth ratio must be sought in socioeconomic conditions applying in the older-settled states. If there were growing constraints on the early marriages that we must assume were formerly common among the rural populations located in eastern areas and growing incentives to family limitation, we can think of the effects as being mitigated as far as national fertility was concerned by the possibility of movement to new land in the west; indeed, on the lines of our Vermont-Genesee model, it could be argued that if more young people had migrated from the older-settled areas, the decline of national fertility might have been postponed for some time.[5] Our next step, clearly, should be to test the hypothesis that rural fertility in the more densely settled states was related to economic opportunities in agriculture.

Here there is a problem of choice: which states should we include in this part of the analysis? It would not be satisfactory simply to take those of the New England, Middle Atlantic, and South Atlantic divisions since, particularly in the earlier part of the period, some of these (for example, New York) contained within their extensive boundaries frontier areas toward which migrants were moving from others (notably, the small New England states). We decided arbitrarily to try cross-section analyses that would include, from each census, observations for those states having adult-farm ratios equal to, or greater than, the median value of this variable for states and territories used at corresponding dates earlier in this work. This is admittedly rough and ready; moreover, it left us with very few observations at the beginning of the century.

For these states in the period 1800-1840, we used Kendall's coefficient of rank correlation to measure the association, at

Table 9. Kendall's Coefficient of Rank Correlation (τ) between
the Rural White Refined Birth Ratio and the Adult-Farm
Ratio in a State, for States Whose Adult-Farm Ratios
Are at a Level of Median or Above, 1800-1840

	Adult-farm ratios based on farm numbers in:	
	1860	*1880*
1800	−.50	−.36
1810	−.50	−.57
1820	−.42	−.64**
1830	−.64**	−.70**
1840	−.64**	−.56**

Note: For explanation of the rural white refined birth ratio, see table
6. Numerators of adult-farm ratios comprise rural adults only. In the
1860 column, states included are (1800) Connecticut, Delaware, Maryland, Massachusetts, New Hampshire, New Jersey, Rhode Island, and
Vermont; (1810) no change; (1820) add South Carolina and Virginia;
(1830) add also Maine and New York; (1840) add also Ohio and
Pennsylvania, delete South Carolina. In the *1880* column, states included are (1800) same as for *1860*; (1810) no change; (1820) add
Maine and New York; (1830) add also Pennsylvania and Virginia;
(1840) add also Ohio.

*Significant at the 5% level.
**Significant at the 1% level.

each census, between rural white refined birth ratios and
adult-farm ratios (whose numerators consist of rural adults
only).[6] Results are given in table 9.

As we should expect, the coefficients are lower than those
calculated for cross sections containing greater numbers of
states and territories, including much more thinly settled
ones, which we gave in chapter 5 (compare table 7, above).
Nevertheless, moderately close inverse associations, significant at the 1 percent level, emerge in the latter part of the
forty-year period (from 1830, when adult-farm ratios are calculated from numbers of rural adults in proportion to farm
numbers in 1860, and alternatively, from 1820, when farm

numbers in 1880 are used). The three lower coefficients for 1800, 1810, and 1820 obtained when adult-farm ratios are based on farm numbers in 1860 are significant just outside the 10 percent level; that for 1810 obtained when adult-farm ratios are based on farm numbers in 1880 is significant just outside the 5 percent level. It is impossible to say just how far we have been successful in removing the more purely demographic influence of internal migration, but almost certainly the results shown in table 9 could be expected to give a more realistic impression of the strength of the relation between the rural white refined birth ratio and relative economic opportunity in agriculture—and clearly something well worth consideration remains.

In our view, a minor deficiency of this method is that it does not relate the rural white refined birth ratio at a given time to the adult-farm ratio at a date ten years earlier, which would seem more appropriate when the children included in child-woman ratios are aged zero to nine. More importantly, it precludes comparisons of the kind we made earlier between the importance of relative densities of agricultural settlement and levels of urbanization as possible determinants of fertility. For this reason, we have recomputed multiple regressions, based on logarithmic transformation of the two explanatory variables, on the model postulated in chapter 4. Once again, however, we have limited the cross sections to those states having adult-farm ratios (now calculated for all adults, urban and rural) at a level of median or above at each date. Table 10 gives coefficients of partial linear correlation between the white refined birth ratio (standardized for 1830 and later) and the logarithm of each of the two variables (which are now lagged by a ten-year interval).

A comparison of results in table 10 and those for all states and territories shown in table 4 indicates that when we confine the regressions to states having adult-farm ratios at a level of median or above, coefficients of partial linear correlation

Table 10. Coefficients of Partial Linear Correlation between the
White Refined Birth Ratio of a State and the Logarithms of
the Adult-Farm Ratio and the Proportion of Urban
Population, for States Whose Adult-Farm Ratios
Are at a Level of Median or Above,
1800-1860

	Adult-Farm Ratio $(r_{y, \log x_1 . \log x_2})$			Proportion of Urban Population $(r_{y, \log x_2 . \log x_1})$		
	(a)	(b)	(c)	(a)	(b)	(c)
1800	-.67	-.74	-.79*	-.24	-.10	.09
1810	-.52	-.79*	-.74	-.63	.02	-.74
1820	-.71*	-.77*	-.89**	.25	.32	-.001
1830	-.81**	-.84**	-.91**	.31	.26	.08
1840	-.83**	-.86**	-.94**	.39	.31	.16
1850	-.53	-.67*	-.72**	.08	.13	-.15
1860		-.62*	-.88**		.13	.44

Note: (a) Adult-farm ratios based on farm numbers in 1850: states included are (1800) Connecticut, Delaware, Maryland, Massachusetts,
New Hampshire, New Jersey, Rhode Island, and Virginia; (1810) no
change; (1820) add South Carolina and Vermont; (1830) add also
New York and Pennsylvania; (1840) add also Maine; (1850) add also
Louisiana and Ohio, delete South Carolina. (b) Adult-farm ratios
based on farm numbers in 1860: states included are (1800) the same
as those listed under (a); (1810) add South Carolina, delete Virginia;
(1820) add also Vermont and Virginia; (1830) add also New York
and Pennsylvania; (1840) add also Maine; (1850) add also Louisiana
and Ohio, delete South Carolina; (1860) add also South Carolina and
Tennessee. (c) Adult-farm ratios based on farm numbers in 1880:
states included are (1800) Connecticut, Delaware, Maryland, Massachusetts, New Hampshire, New Jersey, Rhode Island, and Vermont;
(1810) no change; (1820) add New York and Pennsylvania; (1830)
add also Maine and Virginia; (1840) add also Ohio; (1850) add also
Louisiana; (1860) add also Indiana and Kentucky. The regression
postulated is that stated in chapter 4, p. 27.

*Significant at the 5% level.
**Significant at the 1% level.

between the refined birth ratio and the logarithm of the
adult-farm ratio are affected differently at various dates.
In cross sections for the birth ratios of 1800 and 1810,
they are markedly lower; but in 1820 and 1830 they remain
about the same and all are significant at the 5 percent level
or better. (Indeed, all the coefficients are significant at the
1 percent level in 1830, whether we base adult-farm ratios
on farm numbers in 1850, 1860, or 1880.) In 1840 they
are a little *higher* than they were in cross sections for all
states and territories, and again all are significant at the 1 percent level. Finally, in 1850 and 1860, the partial coefficients
are again broadly the same as in table 4, though inspection
reveals individual discrepancies which are not amenable to
description in a brief commentary of this kind.

When we turn to the coefficients of partial linear correlation between the refined birth ratio and the logarithm of
the proportion of urban population, we find that none is
significant, even at the 5 percent level. Thus the adult-farm
ratio still appears to be much more useful as an explanatory
variable, even when more thinly settled states and territories
with adult-farm ratios less than the median value of this
variable are excluded from the cross sections. However, the
surprising feature of table 10 is that the partial correlation
coefficients between refined birth ratios and urban proportions now show a tendency to become positive.[7] This is true
in fourteen out of a total of twenty instances that are derived from the different cross sections between 1800 and
1860 when adult-farm ratios are based alternatively on farm
numbers in 1850, 1860, and 1880. In table 4, which related
to all states and territories, the corresponding partial coefficients were uniformly negative. We cannot pursue this
further at the present time, but it is an aspect of the analysis
that merits more detailed investigation.

We might be tempted to go on to suggest that the relative
abundance or scarcity of agricultural land was probably a

meaningful socioeconomic determinant of interstate differences of fertility, as distinct from more purely demographic
factors connected with the presence of new settlers in frontier
areas; and in turn, this might make it appear likely that the
downward trend of the national white refined birth ratio
could be ascribed to the growing constraints on marriage
and obstacles to the establishment of new agricultural households arising from increasing densities of settlement in older
states. There is, however, an additional consideration which
should be introduced at this point. We have to ask whether
the *departure* of migrants could have given rise to differences
of fertility among the older states in such a way that birth
ratios tended to be lower in those where adult-farm ratios
were higher and the incentives to outward movement particularly strong—in short, whether it seems reasonable to suppose
that internal migration could have produced significant demographic effects in the east as well as the west. If this were so,
it would follow that the results of cross-section analysis
might be irrelevant to the explanation of national trends of
fertility. At any given time, the whole array of birth ratios
found in different states and territories, new and old, might
be traceable to the effects of internal migration on the demographic characteristics of their populations.

If very high proportions of women aged sixteen to forty-
four migrating between states were married, this would have
helped to raise fertility in areas to which they went; but there
is no obvious reason why it should have led to lower fertility
in the states they left. Women remaining there could still
marry, and as we have suggested, the outflow of migrants
would have had the effect of keeping down pressures on the
land to levels lower than might otherwise have been experienced
thus avoiding the emergence of even greater constraints on the
establishment of new agricultural households. However, it is
likely that internal migration was selective by age and sex,
as well as by marital status. If, as seems probable, younger

adults were prominent among the migrants, this would be
sufficiently taken into account in cross sections for 1830
and later by standardization for differences in the age distribution of women within the childbearing span; and even
with this adjustment, significant inverse associations are still
found between the refined birth ratio of a more densely
settled state and the adult-farm ratio (see tables 9 and 10).
Fortunately, the compositions by sex of the populations
of states and territories can be measured, so that if internal
migration was selective of adult men rather than women,
sex ratios can be introduced as an additional explanatory
variable in our multiple regressions. For populations of
states having adult-farm ratios at a level of median and above,
we should expect to find some evidence of a tendency toward deficiencies in numbers of adult men, more pronounced
among those states whose populations had been significantly
affected by out-migration to other areas—though if we
allowed also for the influence of immigration from overseas, again likely to be selective of adult men and having its
initial impact on particular states containing the ports where
disembarkation typically occurred, no simple pattern of sex
ratios could be deduced a priori. In fact, there were deficiencies
of men, of varying extent, in about half the total number of
observations between 1800 and 1860 for states used in calculating results presented in tables 9 and 10. In these cases,
not all women could hope to be married.[8]

Yasuba refers to the work of H. Yuan T'ien who, by means
of Kendall's coefficient of rank correlation, found significant
positive associations between the sex ratio of a state and its
fertility ratio in cross sections at census dates in the period
1800-1860.[9] T'ien's correlations were calculated from observations for *all* states and territories at given times, and he
made no attempt to eliminate the influence of other possible
determinants of interstate fertility differentials. Moreover,
as Yasuba remarks, the movement over time of the sex ratio

cannot explain the trend of fertility in the United States as a whole during this period. T'ien suggested that demographic factors, including the sex ratio on which he had concentrated his attention, "might have . . . been responsible for the apparent early decline in American fertility" (as measured by the fertility ratio);[10] but although he gave information relating to the sex ratios of individual states and territories, none was provided for the total white population of reproductive age. If we adopt his method of using the age group sixteen to forty-four in the period 1800-1820 and fifteen to forty-nine in the period 1830-60 (for which numbers can be derived directly from the census classifications then in use), sex ratios can be set out as in table 11:

Table 11. Sex Ratios for the Total White Population
of Reproductive Age: United States, 1800-1860

	Number of white males aged 16-44 per 1,000 white females aged 16-44		*Number of white males aged 15-49 per 1,000 white females aged 15-49*
1800	1,014	1830	1,026
1810	1,012	1840	1,046
1820	1,016	1850	1,067
		1860	1,069

Source: Calculated from U.S. censuses.

There is no trend worth considering in the first subperiod; in the second, there is a slight *rise* in the sex ratio, no doubt reflecting the influence of larger-scale immigration from Europe. If, as T'ien believes, there was a *positive* relation between the sex ratio and the fertility ratio, the trend in the former is in the wrong direction if we are seeking to explain a downward trend of the national fertility ratio. On his own hypothesis, T'ien would have to show why fertility declined over time *in spite of* a weak upward movement of the sex ratio.

Nevertheless, the sex ratios of state populations cannot be ignored, especially, it would seem, if our cross sections include observations for states having actual deficiencies of men. What we can get from T'ien is the idea of a positive relation between the sex ratio and (to resume Yasuba's terminology) the refined birth ratio, a relation that T'ien gives some general reasons for assuming is likely to have been curvilinear rather than linear.[11] This he illustrates with two scatter diagrams, for 1800 and 1830, in which the birth ratio of a state or territory is plotted on the vertical axes and the sex ratio on the horizontal. The scatters are convex upward; therefore, they become much more nearly linear if we use the logarithms of sex ratios instead of the natural numbers. We have found this to be so for all census dates in the period 1800-1860 and therefore have been encouraged to proceed with the plan mentioned earlier of adding the logarithm of the sex ratio as a third explanatory variable in multiple regressions of the kind postulated in chapter 4. For states having adult-farm ratios at a level of median or above, in which we are now chiefly interested, coefficients of partial linear correlation between the white refined birth ratio and each of the three supposed explanatory variables are shown in table 12.

Comparison of results in tables 10 and 12 suggests that, in general, our addition of the logarithm of the sex ratio to the regressions has only a minor effect on the partial correlation coefficients between the refined birth ratio and each of the other two variables. Apart from one partial coefficient in 1810, those for the urban proportion are not significant, even at the 5 percent level, and they indicate a mixture of weak positive and negative partial associations, as we found earlier in table 10. It is worth noting that when we include only those states having adult-farm ratios at a level of median or above, this has the incidental effect of confining the cross sections, on the whole, to more highly urbanized states; thus

Table 12. Coefficients of Partial Linear Correlation between the White Refined Birth Ratio of a State and the Logarithms of the Adult-Farm Ratio, the Proportion of Urban Population, and the Sex Ratio, for States Whose Adult-Farm Ratios Are at a Level of Median or Above, 1800-1860

	Adult-Farm Ratio $(r_{y, \log x_1, \log x_2, \log x_3})$			Proportion of Urban Population $(r_{y, \log x_2, \log x_1, \log x_3})$			Sex Ratio $(r_{y, \log x_3, \log x_1, \log x_2})$		
	(a)	(b)	(c)	(a)	(b)	(c)	(a)	(b)	(c)
1800	-.62	-.65	-.56	.04	.08	.11	.52	.41	.19
1810	-.33	-.39	-.20	-.67	-.14	-.83*	.73	.66	.61
1820	-.76*	-.76*	-.69	.19	.19	-.25	.88**	.84**	.62
1830	-.83**	-.87**	-.91**	.17	.09	-.01	.33	.36	.17
1840	-.82**	-.82**	-.91**	.30	.20	-.04	.58	.42	.60*
1850	-.47	-.61*	-.69*	-.01	.08	-.05	.24	.12	-.21
1860		-.59*	-.87**		.07	.42		.32	.02

Note: (a) Adult-farm ratios based on farm numbers in 1850. (b) Adult-farm ratios based on farm numbers in 1860. (c) Adult-farm ratios based on farm numbers in 1880. States included are those having adult-farm ratios at a level of median or above, as listed under (a), (b), and (c) in note to table 10. The regression postulated is $Y_{(t)} = a + \beta_1 \log X_{1(t-10)} + \beta_2 \log X_{2(t-10)} + \beta_3 \log X_{3(t-10)} + \epsilon$, where $Y_{(t)}$ is the white refined birth ratio in a state (standardized for 1830 and later); $X_{1(t-10)}$ is the adult-farm ratio at a date ten years earlier; $X_{2(t-10)}$ is the proportion of urban population (in percentage points) at a date ten years earlier; and $X_{3(t-10)}$ is the sex ratio at a date ten years earlier. (Sex ratios as defined in table 11 cannot be calculated for 1790; therefore, the sex ratios of states in 1800 have been used *both* in the 1800 and 1810 regressions.)
    *Significant at the 5% level.
  **Significant at the 1% level.

when adult-farm ratios are based on farm numbers in 1880, the regression for the refined birth ratios of 1860 includes all states whose urban proportions were greater than 10 percent in 1850, with the single exception of Missouri. The range of urban proportions in this cross section is from 1.9 percent in Vermont to 55.6 percent in Rhode Island.[12] Yet the coefficient of partial linear correlation between the standardized refined birth ratio and the logarithm of the urban proportion is computed at +.42. That for the logarithm of the adult-farm ratio, in the same regression, is −.87, significant at the 1 percent level. This admittedly is an extreme case, as inspection of table 12 will show, but it is difficult to avoid an impression that, generally in this context, the proportion of urban population is of little value as an explanatory variable.

If we turn now to the coefficients of partial linear correlation between the refined birth ratio and the logarithm of the adult-farm ratio, it is noticeable that elimination of the influence of the sex ratio has most effect early in the period. The partial association between the birth ratio and the adult-farm ratio is slightly weakened in 1800 and considerably affected in 1810. From 1820 onward the pattern of partial coefficients remains much the same, whether or not the sex ratio is included in the regressions. It seems likely, therefore, that the inverse association between fertility and density of agricultural settlement (which comes to the same thing as a positive association between fertility and the availability of easily accessible land) may reflect a real socioeconomic relationship and not merely a more superficial relation arising from the effects of internal migration on the compositions by sex of state populations. Yasuba's emphasis on the importance of economic opportunities in agriculture is supported, though by different means.

To borrow a passage from Yasuba, but adapting it to relate to a different variable: if increasing scarcity of good, cheap

land in older states was the major force in reducing fertility
in this period, we should expect not only that those states
with higher adult-farm ratios would have lower fertility but
also that the states that experienced a greater *increase* in
adult-farm ratios would show a greater *decline* in fertility.[13]
We have made such an analysis, first, for changes over the
period 1800-1840 in the rural white refined birth ratios of
the states of Connecticut, Delaware, Maryland, Massachusetts,
New Hampshire, New Jersey, Rhode Island, and Vermont,
which are included at both dates in table 9. These are the
states that had ratios of rural adults to farm numbers in 1860
and 1880 at a level of median or above in the cross section
for 1800. Kendall's coefficient of rank correlation between
the percentage increase in the adult-farm ratio (calculated
for rural adults) and the absolute decrease in the rural white
refined birth ratio of a state is .57 if we base adult-farm ratios
on farm numbers in 1860 and .50 if we use farm numbers in
1880. The first of these two coefficients is significant just
outside the 5 percent level (6.2%); the second, just outside
the 10 percent level (10.8%). The coefficients remain un-
changed if the percentage decrease in the rural birth ratio is
used instead of the absolute decrease.

   In these correlations Kendall's coefficient is weakened
chiefly by the ranking of one state, New Jersey, which is
the sole clearly aberrant area. If it were dropped from the
calculation, the coefficients for the remaining seven states
would rise to .90 and .81 respectively, with enhanced levels
of significance. We do not wish to interfere arbitrarily with
the data in this way, but perhaps a better idea of the strength
of the association can be obtained from a linear regression,
for all eight states, of the absolute decrease in the rural white
refined birth ratio on the percentage increase in the (rural)
adult-farm ratio between 1800 and 1840. When adult-farm
ratios are based on farm numbers in 1860, the correlation
coefficient is .71; if we use farm numbers in 1880, it is

.72. Both coefficients are significant at the 5 percent level.[14]

This regression takes no account of the possible influence of changes in the sex ratios of the eight states in question. To remedy this, we have computed coefficients of partial linear correlation between the absolute change in the white refined birth ratio of a state, 1800-1840, and change in the logarithms of the explanatory variables, including the sex ratio, postulated in the multiple regression stated in the note to table 12. Here the numerators of adult-farm ratios comprise all adults, urban as well as rural; but it happens that when farm numbers in 1880 are used as denominators, the same eight states have adult-farm ratios at a level of median or above at the beginning of the period. (This is not so if we divide by farm numbers in 1860, for in this case Virginia replaces Vermont.) If then we use adult-farm ratios based on farm numbers in 1880, the partial correlation coefficient between the change of the birth ratio and change of the logarithm of the adult-farm ratio is -.79 (which is significant at the 10 percent level but not at 5 percent); that for change of the logarithm of the urban proportion -.04; and that for change of the logarithm of the sex ratio -.31. Neither of the latter two is significant at anything even approaching an acceptable level, and the partial correlation coefficient between the change of the birth ratio and change of the logarithm of the sex ratio has a sign opposite from that which we should expect a priori.[15] The adult-farm ratio still appears more useful than the proportion of urban population as an explanatory variable, and our analysis helps to support the hypothesis that it may have been a meaningful socioeconomic determinant of changes in fertility.[16]

This impression would be strengthened if we considered, for each of these states, the absolute change of the birth ratio over a rather shorter period, from 1800 to 1830. In this case,

coefficients of partial linear correlation with change of the
logarithms of the adult-farm ratio, urban proportion, and
sex ratio (which it will be remembered relate to dates ten
years earlier in our multiple regressions)[17] are -.91 (significant at the 2 percent level), -.51, and -.58 respectively.[18]
On the other hand, if we again use the same eight states,
and adult-farm ratios based on farm numbers in 1880, corresponding partial coefficients for change over the period
1830-60 are quite markedly different: -.34, -.13, and
-.04.[19] The square of the coefficient of multiple correlation plummets from .867 (1800-1830) to .133 (1830-60).

As far as the partial association between change of the
birth ratio and change of the adult-farm ratio is concerned,
these results seem to fit well enough with Yasuba's conclusion, reached by different means, that "there is a downward trend in the degree of association between the increase
in population density [per 1,000 acres of arable land] and
the decline in the refined birth ratio."[20] The adult-farm ratio
emerges as a useful variable to explain change of the birth
ratios of the eight states over the period 1800-1830, or even
1800-1840, but fares less well thereafter. Here two comments
are relevant.

First, by continuing to confine the analysis to the same
eight states in the period 1830-60 we are applying a stricter
test to our hypotheses than was used for the period 1800-
1830. In a sense, results for the two periods might be regarded as more nearly comparable if for the second, as for
the first, we included all states with adult-farm ratios at a
level of median or above at its beginning—that is, 1830, which
allowing for a ten-year time lag means taking the more densely
settled states according to the adult-farm ratios of 1820. To
do this, we have to add observations for four more states;
when adult-farm ratios are based on farm numbers in 1880,
these are Maine, New York, Pennsylvania, and Virginia.[21]
Coefficients of partial linear correlation between the abso-

lute change of the refined birth ratio of a state and change of the logarithms of the adult-farm ratio, urban proportion, and sex ratio over the period 1830-60 are $-.71$ (significant at the 5 percent level), $-.22$, and $-.15$.[22] The square of the coefficient of multiple correlation is .515. On the face of things, this is a more satisfactory result;[23] but there is still a clear weakening of the partial association between the decrease of the refined birth ratio and the increase of the logarithm of the adult-farm ratio and a reduction in the multiple correlation coefficient.

Second, if the adult-farm ratio does not appear as useful a variable to explain change of the refined birth ratio in more densely settled states after 1830 or 1840, the proportion of urban population shows little or no sign of taking its place. Whichever way we take our measures, the partial association between the decrease of the refined birth ratio and the increase of the logarithm of the urban proportion remains weaker than the association with change in the density of agricultural settlement.

Immigration and American Fertility Ratios
before the Civil War

This chapter will discuss the possible effect of international
migration on American birth ratios before the Civil War—
initially, not the separate birth ratios of states and territories
but the national white refined birth ratio. The influence of
immigration can be expected to have been felt most clearly
toward the mid-century, since the rate of gross immigration
(number of arrivals per 1,000 of American population) increased sharply in the 1840s and early 1850s, reaching a peak
in 1854.[1] Our interest, therefore, is chiefly in these two
decades.

First it will be necessary to define our problem more carefully. We have discussed two factors which may have influenced fertility: economic opportunities in agriculture, and
industrialization-urbanization. Insofar as immigration caused
the population of the United States to grow more quickly
than it would otherwise have done, it would probably have
had some effect—though perhaps only slight—on both of
these determinants; in Yasuba's words, "by reducing the
availability of easily accessible land and facilitating industrialization and urbanization."[2] This, however, is not the question
we propose to take up. Ours can be stated in this way. Suppose there is a given total population in the United States.
Hypothetically, it might be composed wholly of native
Americans, or partly of native Americans and partly of the
foreign-born. How would the standardized refined birth ratio
of the mixed native and foreign-born population be likely
to differ from that which would have applied in a population
of the same size but consisting entirely of native Americans?

Most generalizations about the effects of immigration into
the United States have been based on data relating to the late

nineteenth and early twentieth centuries, a time when increasing proportions of the country's immigrants were being drawn from southern and eastern Europe. If it is true that "immigrants tend to carry over the family-building patterns of their native communities,"[3] their fertility at this time (which is to be understood as age-specific fertility) may well have been higher than that of native Americans, thus tending to raise the level in the United States above that which would have been found in a wholly native population of the same size. (Insofar as higher proportions of first-generation immigrants than of native Americans tended to be concentrated in unskilled or semiskilled occupations,[4] immigrant-native fertility differences could have been further reinforced. However, from the point of view of national fertility, allowance would have to be made for the lower fertility of natives who were "floated" into more skilled work, thus improving their economic status as a result of the availability of immigrants to supply part of the economy's needs for unskilled labor.) On the other hand, in the period before the Civil War, immigrants came predominantly from northern and northwestern Europe. Here fertility almost certainly was lower, on the whole, than in southern and eastern Europe; and moreover, American fertility would then have been higher than it was in the late nineteenth century. It is by no means clear that age-specific fertility in Ireland, Germany, England, Scotland, or the Scandinavian countries was higher than that in the United States during the 1840s and 1850s: the presumption would be to the contrary. It looks as if the immigrants were coming from areas in which family-building patterns were lower, not higher, than in the United States.

All we can do is compare estimates of crude birth rates, placing them where possible against estimates of total fertility rates given by Coale and Zelnik.[5] In 1850 the white birth rate in the United States was probably about forty-three to forty-four per thousand, while the total fertility rate is estimated at 5.42. In England, Wales, and Scotland, corresponding figures would be about thirty-four per thousand for the crude birth rate and just under 5 for the total fertility rate; for Sweden, a birth rate of about thirty-two to thirty-three per thousand, with a total fertility rate rather lower than the English—say about 4.5.[6] The German birth rate in the 1840s, prior to a downward fluctuation evident in series for the early 1850s, was about thirty-six per thousand.[7]

Estimates for Ireland merit more detailed comment, not only because the Irish were the most important element among the foreign-born population of the United States in the mid-nineteenth century but also because it was once suggested by K. H. Connell that Irish fertility was much higher than the English.[8] Possibly this is an impression that many would still be prepared to accept. However, Connell agreed shortly afterward with a reviewer, R. C. Geary, that this idea had been based on an error made in extracting data from the Irish census of 1841, by which figures he had given "for the number of children under 1 and under 5 . . . relate in fact to the number under 2 and under 6." He now accepted that a corrected figure for the number of children aged zero to four per 1,000 women aged fifteen to forty-four "no longer supports the conclusion that fertility was remarkably higher in Ireland than in England";[9] and more recently this has been interpreted by Michael Drake as a recognition that "there was no difference in fertility between the two countries."[10]

It was noted by the commissioners of the Irish census of 1841, the last before the famine, that the country had no general registers of births, either ecclesiastical or civil.[11] (In England, of course, there was civil registration of births from the late 1830s onward, gradually improving in accuracy.) For this reason, when comparing Ireland and England, it seems best to confine our attention to child-woman ratios (follow-

ing Yasuba, we have called these birth ratios). Drake gives
figures for two such Irish ratios in 1841: children under one
and under five per 1,000 women aged fifteen to forty-four.
However, we feel there are grounds for treating the former
with some reserve. The Irish census of 1841 lists ages in
months (1, 2, 3, . . . 12), and then ages in years (2, 3, 4, . . .
right through to 113), giving a number against each.[12] Strict-
ly interpreted, since there is no age zero months, the first
group must be regarded as being aged less than one month;
and those aged "twelve months" as being eleven months
and less than twelve months. But there is an immense concentration at "twelve months": 158,958 children as compared, for example, with only 7,798 at "eleven months."
Clearly the 158,958 children at "twelve months" would
have included three sorts: some whose ages were properly
given as being in their twelfth month but not yet one year
of age; others, probably, whose ages were near their twelfth
month but not yet in it, who were wrongly included in that
group; and a large number aged one and less than two years,
who again got into the "twelve months" group because there
was nowhere else for them to go in a table of ages which,
regrettably, lacked one of its necessary classes.[13] If Connell
was originally in error when he included the whole of these
158,958 children in the number aged less than one year,
Drake seems also to have slipped into error by leaving them
all out of his numerator—some should have been allocated
to the under-one class. Probably this measure is better ignored.

We have therefore limited our comparison to numbers of children aged zero to four per 1,000 women aged fifteen to forty-
four, though even here it is necessary to give an estimate for
Ireland instead of a ratio calculated directly and literally
from the census of 1841. This is because the numbers reported at ages within the zero-to-four group make it seem
likely that those aged zero ("one month" + "two months"

+ . . . "eleven months" = 202,466) and aged one ("twelve months" = 158,958) were *both* very seriously understated in the report. To see this, all we need do is compare these figures with those for age two (230,804), age three (218,149), and age four (219,148). Only a spectacular fall of births at the end of the 1830s could have produced such an erosion at the base of the Irish age pyramid; or alternatively, it would have needed a freak wave of deaths hitting selectively at very young children (aged zero and one) about the time of the census.[14] Moreover, the missing children appear to have been wholly lost in some way and not recorded in error at an adjacent age. Thus the total number of children aged zero to four reported in the Irish census of 1841 was 1,029,525, compared with a greater number—1,076,205— aged five to nine. If we are to judge by census figures for England and Wales, or Scotland, in 1841 and 1851, the former group ought to have exceeded the latter by about 9-12 percent. Again, in 1861, Irish children aged zero to four exceeded those aged five to nine by 13 percent.[15]

To obtain a rough estimate of the number of Irish children aged zero to four in 1841, it seemed easiest to take the number aged five to nine and add a round 10 percent. This gave 1,183,826 children aged zero to four as against 1,934,298 women aged fifteen to forty-four, or a ratio of 612 per 1,000. Our comparison now is shown in table 13.

It could be, of course, that the underenumeration of children relative to that of women was greater in Ireland than in England or that infant and child mortality was higher there. Either of these things, if established, would affect our interpretation of the two birth ratios between which there is some difference in favor of Ireland but not a large one. Again, it is possible that Irish fertility in the 1830s and early 1840s was already being abnormally constrained by forces that were to make themselves felt with much greater severity after the famine. But these would be refinements.

Table 13. Comparison of Irish Fertility Ratio with
that of England and Wales

	Ireland	England and Wales
Children aged 0-4 per 1,000 women aged 15-44	612 (est. 1841)	553 (1841), 554 (1851)
Ever-married women as a percentage of total women in age group 46-55 (Ireland) and 45-54 (England and Wales)	87.5 (1841)	87.8 (1851)

Source: Irish fertility ratio estimated as described in text, based on "Census of Ireland, 1841," p. 488; and percentage ever married calculated from pp. 438-39. England and Wales: calculated from Mitchell, *Abstract of British Historical Statistics*, pp. 12, 15. (English figures for 1841 are said to be approximate ones only.)

The plain fact is that the American ratio of white children aged zero to four per 1,000 women aged fifteen to forty-four in 1840 is given by W. S. Thompson and P. K. Whelpton as 797,[16] which is 30 percent higher than the Irish estimate for 1841 and 44 percent higher than the English ratio. There is nothing here to make us revise our earlier suggestion that fertility in the countries from which American immigrants were being drawn in the 1840s and 1850s was lower than that in the United States—though the nature of the response of Irish immigrant fertility (or English) to American economic and social conditions after arrival is another question, especially since, in the circumstances of the time, it would have been easier, presumably, to revise family-building patterns upward rather than downward.

Yasuba's discussion relates to "fertility" measured in a special way: not by annual births per 1,000 women in given age groups, as we would measure age-specific fertility if the data were available, but by numbers of children aged zero to nine per 1,000 women aged sixteen to forty-four. Here there could be an additional factor to be considered in connection with the *immediate* effects of a large intake of immigrants on the American white refined birth ratio. How did the refined birth ratio of immigrants, at the time of their disembarkation, compare with that of native Americans? Fortunately, there is some information on this question, given by the Superintendent of the Seventh Census. In his *Report* there is a "Statement showing the sexes and ages of 245,336 immigrants who arrived at New York, Boston, and New Orleans during the year ending September 30, 1850, compared with the same number of native white inhabitants of the United States."[17] The refined birth ratio of the native white Americans, in what was apparently about a 1 percent sample,[18] works out at 1,592 children under ten years of age per 1,000 women between fifteen and forty years. (This looks about right, though possibly a little higher than we should expect, even after making a rough allowance for the unusually narrow age group used in the denominator.) The immigrants included 32,184 children under ten years of age and 68,253 women between fifteen and forty years, giving a ratio of 472 per 1,000 or only about 30 percent of the native-American figure.

Clearly, any impression we might have of immigrant women arriving with large numbers of children would be wrong. On disembarkation, they had many fewer than did native-American women aged fifteen to forty—at least if the year 1850 was at all representative of conditions in the mid-century, with which we are at present chiefly concerned. But we can do more than this, since the Eighth Census of 1860 gives a distribution of ages on arrival of an aggregate of 5,272,486 passengers who entered the United States between 1820 and 1860.[19] These are in five-year groups to age thirty-nine, with a final group recorded as forty and over; each is cross-classified by sex. The table includes both native citizens returning to their own country and passengers of foreign birth, "but since the foreigners are far more numerous, the result will exhibit very nearly the relative number at each age of the foreign passengers." The ratio of children aged zero to nine to women aged fifteen to thirty-nine is 603 per 1,000; the ratio per 1,000 women aged fifteen to forty would be of the order of 590-595. This is higher than the immigrant child-woman ratio we obtained for 1850 but still far below the sample native-American figure for that year of 1,592 children aged zero to nine per 1,000 women aged fifteen to forty. Over four-fifths of the arrivals in question took place in the 1840s and 1850s.[20]

We then have to ask whether the difference between the native-American birth ratio and that of immigrants on arrival was attributable solely to the particular distribution of immigrant women over the childbearing ages and thus could be removed by standardizing the immigrant child-woman ratio to the age distribution of American women in a given year. (So far we have used the year 1860.) If we work in terms of three of the age groups enumerated in United States censuses from 1830 onward—fifteen to nineteen, twenty to twenty-nine, and thirty to thirty-nine—and apply the same fertility table as was used to standardize American refined birth ratios,[21] it quickly becomes clear that the only way in which we could convert the unstandardized immigrant child-woman ratio on arrival into a standardized one approaching the native-American ratio would be by allocating a large proportion of the immigrant women to the fifteen-to-nineteen group—perhaps about three-quarters or more, depending on how we distributed the remainder between the other two age groups. In fact, the ratio for those arriving over the period 1820-60, when standardized, increases from 603 children aged zero to nine per 1,000 women aged fifteen to thirty-nine to 636; or, to revert to our first measure, if we assume that the women who arrived in the year ended 30 September 1850 had an age distribution similar to that of women who entered over

the whole period 1820-60, the ratio of 472 children aged
zero to nine per 1,000 women aged fifteen to forty rises to
about five hundred.[22] Thus the standardized birth ratio of
immigrant women at time of disembarkation in the United
States was very much lower than the native-American ratio—
in round figures, no more than 30-40 percent of it.[23]

We can do no more than list possible reasons for this difference. Thus, while it seems unlikely, on general grounds,
that international migration would have included very large
numbers of single women, it may have been selective of
women who had married only shortly before leaving Europe,
with little time for childbearing before arrival in America.
(If this were so, the child-woman ratio among immigrants
on disembarkation would tell us little about their future
potential as mothers in the United States.) Again, those who
had already been married for some time and produced children in Europe may have lost a disproportionate number
by death compared with American families. We have to remember that the recent experience of some, most notably
in Ireland, would have included famine or near-famine conditions.[24] And finally, even if international migration was
not naturally selective but simply transferred a representative sample of women, including single women, from western
Europe (an unlikely assumption), a higher average age at
first marriage than that obtaining in the United States might
still have played a part. In this case there would have been
more single women among all immigrant women of reproductive age than among American women.

In considering the effects of immigration on the standardized
white refined birth ratio of the United States, it is easiest to
think in terms of a given cohort of immigrant women entering in a particular year, together with the children who ac-
companied them on arrival and others who subsequently
would have been added to their families. Immediately on
disembarkation, the immigrants would reduce the standard-

ized refined birth ratio; or to make the point more carefully in terms of the problem defined at the beginning of this chapter, a population of given size, urbanized to the same degree, containing a proportion of newly arrived immigrants would have had a somewhat lower standardized refined birth ratio than one composed wholly of native Americans. Since there were women immigrating in every year, this immediate effect would be a continuing one, annually renewed on a greater or smaller scale in accordance with fluctuations in the rate of new arrivals. However, we must remember that the intake in any year was always very small in proportion to the American female population of reproductive age.

New entrants would have exerted a continuing effect but not necessarily a cumulative one. Although the standardized refined birth ratio of a given cohort of immigrants at time of arrival was much lower than that of native Americans, it would have risen during the early years of that cohort's residence in the United States, thus reducing the difference—perhaps even eliminating it or creating a difference in the opposite direction. We could expect a sharp rise to have occurred particularly if the main cause of the lowness of immigrant birth ratios on arrival was an element of selection favoring, among wives, a high proportion only recently married. As the duration of their marriages increased, so would the number of their children aged zero to nine.[25]

Although we cannot be sure, this consideration suggests that the effects of new entry may have been most significant for results derived from the Seventh Census of 1850. We have seen that the rate of gross immigration (number of arrivals per 1,000 of American population) rose sharply in the 1840s and early 1850s, reaching a peak in 1854. There was a similar movement in the rate of what we might call white reproductive female immigration (estimated number of female immigrants aged fifteen to thirty-nine per 1,000 American white females of the same age). If we estimate female immigrants aged fifteen to thirty-nine by the method already described (note 24 to this chapter), we can select figures for the years 1828, 1839, 1849, and 1859 to typify relative levels of entry just before the censuses of 1830, 1840, 1850, and 1860. (In 1829 the ages of a considerable number of arrivals were not reported; therefore it has been necessary to use 1828 in its place.) If we compare these with the American white female population aged fifteen to thirty-nine as shown in the four censuses, we obtain rates of white reproductive female immigration of 2.3, 5.9, 19.2, and 8.4 per 1,000 respectively.

This makes it seem likely that results obtained from the census of 1850 would have been most affected by immigration, but it should be noted that our method of measurement is not wholly satisfactory. No allowance has been made for any change there may have been in the difference between the native-American standardized refined birth ratio and that of immigrants on arrival; more importantly, it would have been preferable to take a weighted average of the intakes over a period of years before each census, giving greatest weight to immigrants whose arrival took place immediately before an enumeration and progressively diminishing weights to others whose earlier arrival gave more time for family building before the census in question. But it would be difficult to know what weights to apply, and in any case the general impression seems fairly clear. Given the rapid falling away of immigration from its peak in 1854, it is hardly reasonable to suppose that results taken from the census of 1860 could have been as much affected as those in 1850.

It seems impossible to say whether, after a sufficient interval of time, the standardized refined birth ratio of a given cohort of immigrants would have been likely to have fallen short of, equaled, or exceeded the native-American ratio.[26] All we can do is list a number of relevant considerations. (1) If international migration was selective of married women rather than single (as we have suggested was probably true of internal migration), it might have been that the proportion of married women among total immigrant women of childbearing age was higher than that among native Americans. Other things being equal, this would tend, given time, to produce a standardized refined birth ratio higher than the native-American ratio. (2) Immigration is known to have been selective of adult males rather than females.[27] It is possible that foreign-born men sought wives chiefly, though not of course exclusively, among foreign-born women; if so, their competition could have contributed to produce relatively high proportions married and hence high fertility. (3) Immigrant women who had married before arrival in the United States may have done so at the higher average age we should expect to have been characteristic of northern and northwestern Europe. Assuming that fecundity declines as a woman's age increases, then other things being equal this would tend to produce a lower standardized refined birth ratio among foreign-born women than among native Americans. (4) If immigrants from northern and northwestern Europe were more accustomed to control intramarital fertility and if they retained a European attitude toward family size, this again would limit their standardized refined birth ratio, tending to hold it below the native-American ratio. (5) If immigrant women had lost a disproportionate number of children by differential child mortality in Europe compared with the United States, this would have tended to keep their standardized refined birth ratio below the native American. A part—possibly a large part— of the difference might have been made up by new conceptions in the United States, but there remains a question whether differential child mortality in Europe (if it applied) could have been fully compensated in this way.

What the net effect of these conflicting influences would have been, given time for full adjustment of immigrant

standardized refined birth ratios from the very low levels
estimated on arrival, is anyone's guess. Perhaps the first
factor we have mentioned—a tendency of immigration to
be selective of married women rather than single—would
have been sufficient to produce somewhat higher fertility
among foreign-born women compared with native American. However, knowing so little, we should at least be prepared to contemplate a possibility that immigrant standardized refined birth ratios could have remained lower than
native American in the period before the Civil War, even
with time for additional family building after arrival in the
United States, and not risen higher (for given cohorts), as
we might otherwise have been tempted to assume on the
basis of experience in the late nineteenth and early twentieth
centuries.

How does this bear on the cross-section analysis discussed
earlier, which was based on observation of differences between the white refined birth ratios of states and territories
at given times? The point coming immediately to mind is
that the relative levels of state birth ratios could have been
disturbed to some extent, thus affecting the correlations
with factors we have considered as possible determinants of
fertility. This follows from the fact that immigrants were
distributed very unevenly.[28] Their proportions to total white
population were high in the northeast, especially in the states
of New York, Massachusetts, and Rhode Island, where standardized refined birth ratios were relatively low. Immigrant
birth ratios on disembarkation would have been even lower,
but given time for family building after arrival, the fertility
of the foreign-born may well have exceeded that of native
Americans.[29] The effect on the birth ratio of a northeastern
state as measured in a particular census could have gone
either way, depending on the pattern over time of immigration—whether, for example, there had been a steeply rising
influx just before the census, as there was in the late 1840s—

and on how rapidly children were added to immigrant
families after arrival in the United States.

The likely effect appears less equivocal in western states
and territories, where fertility was higher than in the northeast. Thus it is possible that the entry of overseas immigrants
into Wisconsin and Minnesota, where about a third of the
population was foreign-born in the mid-century, may help
to explain, partly at least, the unexpectedly low standardized refined birth ratios found there in 1850 and 1860.
Measured as children aged zero to nine per 1,000 women
aged sixteen to forty-four, these were then at levels around
fifteen hundred, which is a good deal less than those in some
other areas at early stages of their development. For example,
Indiana and Illinois had unstandardized birth ratios of over
2,200 in 1810 and standardized ratios still above this figure
in 1830.[30] In general, we should expect the effects of differences in the proportions of immigrants to the total white
populations of states and territories to have been small, but
in some instances they could have been significant.

There is a final point we wish to make in this context,
though relating chiefly now to internal migration within
the United States. At the end of his book Yasuba notes that
there might have been other major determinants of fertility
as well as those he had analyzed. "In fact," he says "the
relatively low refined birth ratios in new states and territories
in 1860 compared with the refined birth ratios in new areas
in 1800 suggest that other factors—for example, propagation
of the knowledge of contraceptive techniques and decline
in the importance of religious inhibitions—may have been
at work."[31] To these conjectures we have just added another:
in some new states and territories at the end of the period,
and especially perhaps at the time of the Seventh Census of
1850, an influence may have been exerted by relatively large
numbers of overseas immigrants. This would apply particularly if the foreign-born settlers were newly arrived from

Europe and not members of earlier cohorts of immigrants, resident longer in the United States, who had gradually made their way westward with time for family building in the process. Is it reasonable to suppose that a given cohort of internal migrants, now thought of as American citizens from farther east, could have had a similar influence on the standardized refined birth ratios of new states and territories?

So far we have emphasized the likely effect of internal migration in contributing to relatively high refined birth ratios in thinly settled areas at an early stage of occupation. This could be expected if internal migration was selective of married women rather than single, thus tending to produce very high proportions of wives among all women aged sixteen to forty-four. We suggested also that these high proportions of married women would probably have declined over time, with a corresponding effect on birth ratios, as increasing numbers of young people growing up in the newer areas entered the sixteen-to-forty-four age group and so reduced the relative importance of adult internal migrants who had arrived in the first wave of settlement of formerly empty territory (see above, p. 49ff.). Again, it has been noted that from among wives generally, internal migration may have been selective of those only recently married—we have no presumptive evidence to support this idea, as we have in the case of international migration, but on general grounds it seems reasonable (see note 25 to this chapter). If so, we should expect the standardized refined birth ratio of a given cohort of internal migrants not to have been particularly high on arrival and then to have risen. Thus, as those first settling a new territory added to their families, there may well have been an interval during which the rising number of their children aged zero to nine counterbalanced, or more than counterbalanced, the declining tendency of the refined birth ratio which would otherwise have been experienced (because of a decline in the proportion of married women among all women aged sixteen to forty-four), thereby giving an initial impetus to stability of the birth ratio or even an upward movement. Effects of this kind could have been produced in any area being newly occupied in the course of westward expansion, and as with international migration, their net influence on the standardized refined birth ratio recorded in an early census for a new state or territory would depend on the particular "mix" applying at that time. These are fine shades of conjecture: to simplify, we can say that except perhaps at the very beginning of occupation of new areas, the overall effect of internal migration would have been to give relatively high birth ratios in the early stage of settlement of places toward which it was directed.

However, there might also have been trend factors operating over the period, so that although internal migration continued to lift the level of birth ratios in new states and territories, it did so to a diminishing extent. By the mid-century, demographic conditions in the northeast of the United States would not have been all that much different from those in northern and northwestern Europe. Thus migrants from old-settled eastern states may have included increasing proportions of women married at higher ages, and if fecundity tends to decline with age, this could have had some effect in limiting the levels of western standardized refined birth ratios. Probably it would have been only slight. Again, it is just possible that the families of older married couples moving west (and there must have been some older migrants, in spite of a tendency toward selectivity by age) would have included a greater admixture of daughters aged sixteen and over still remaining single. More importantly perhaps, acceptance of contraception by migrants from the east and ideas they entertained regarding a proper family size could have been influenced by customs in their original home states. Perhaps these ideas would have been jettisoned in the more thinly settled western regions to which they went, and to a considerable extent this seems likely to have taken place. But the adjustment to different economic and social conditions may not have been complete, so that, at least in some measure, attitudes to family size which had emerged in more densely settled eastern states were diffused elsewhere.

Rural and Urban Components of the Decline in the American Fertility Ratio

We return to Potter who, it will be remembered (see above, p. 2), has said he is not convinced by Yasuba's conclusion regarding the primary importance of the relative plenty or scarcity of easily accessible land as a determinant of fertility—a conclusion which, as Potter recognizes by quoting from Yasuba's work, was applied by him particularly to "the first few decades of the nineteenth century."[1] Potter offers a very brief discussion in which, without explanation, he narrows the question to make it relate to the period 1830-60 instead of 1800-1860 and then sums up in the following way:

> The findings have to remain inconclusive. But the evidence still seems to support the view that industrialization and urbanization, with the accompaniment of higher living standards and greater social expectations (but possibly also higher infant mortality), were the main reasons for the declining rate of population growth [rate of natural increase?], either through the postponement of marriage or the restriction of family size.[2]

The positive evidence Potter offers in favor of his own emphasis on industrialization and urbanization depends mainly on an observation, which he describes as "preliminary and superficial," that in the period 1830-60 the cities of Philadelphia and New York, the more urbanized counties within Massachusetts, and the more urbanized districts in some other states "all show a distinctly lower proportion of children than the average for the state."[3] "These ratios," he adds, "do not in themselves prove a lower fertility rate. They might indicate a higher rate of infant mortality in urbanized areas."

So far we have no objection, but he goes on immediately to
a proposition we cannot accept: "if, as many writers have
assumed, there was a decline in the birth rate, it seems to
have been heavily concentrated in the urbanized counties
and above all in the industrializing areas of the North-East;
the decline elsewhere may have been so slight as to be
negligible." This has too many things against it: the graphs,
based on Yasuba's tables and shown above in figure 1 where
the downward trends appear to have been much more general,
affecting largely rural states and territories as well as more
highly urbanized states in the northeast; Yasuba's failure
and our own to obtain close inverse associations between
refined birth ratios and urban proportions by means of
"standardized rank correlation" or Kendall's coefficient
of partial rank correlation (though on these measures, for
cross sections including all states and territories, urban proportions seem to offer more of a challenge to densities of
agricultural settlement as determinants of interstate differences of fertility near the end of the period under review);
our failure to obtain significant coefficients of partial linear
correlation between refined birth ratios and urban proportions after logarithmic transformation of the explanatory
variables (either for cross sections covering all states and
territories or for those including only the more densely
settled states); the generally downward trends of the *rural*
white refined birth ratios of states and territories during the
period 1800-1840 shown in table 6.

We can now add one more, since it is possible, as a departure from the methods of analysis we have used so far,
to measure in a statistical sense the respective contributions
to the total change in the American white refined birth ratio
of (1) the decline in the rural refined birth ratio, (2) the decline in the urban refined birth ratio, and (3) the rural-to-
urban shift of population. These contributions can be calculated from the estimates of rural and urban fertility ratios

made by Grabill, Kiser, and Whelpton.[4] Unfortunately, the
estimates can be made only for the period 1800-1840 (and
again from 1910), but with some guesswork it is possible in
a rough way to extend them to the years 1840-60.

The refined birth ratio used by Grabill, Kiser, and Whelpton
(children aged zero to four per 1,000 white women aged
twenty to forty-four) rises slightly between 1800 and 1810,
so it may be best to confine the analysis in the first place to
the period 1810-40. It should be noted that although these
writers give estimates of the national, rural, and urban birth
ratios in 1810 and 1840, they do not show the rural-urban
proportions applicable to the white population at each date.
Those published in *Historical Statistics of the United States*
do not fill the gap, since they are for the total population,
white and nonwhite. However, the national white refined
birth ratio is a weighted average of the rural and urban ratios;
once we know these three figures at each date, the implicit
weights can be derived. For 1810 and 1840 they can be
shown as follows (Bureau of the Census rural-urban proportions of the total population are included for comparison):

		Rural	*Urban*
1810	White, implicit weights	90.91%	9.09%
1810	Bureau of the Census,		
	1940 urban-rural definition	92.74%	7.26%
1840	White, implicit weights	85.22%	14.78%
1840	Bureau of the Census,		
	1940 urban-rural definition	89.19%	10.81%

An evaluation of the components of the decline in the
national fertility ratio between 1810 and 1840 is given in
table 14. (As Grabill, Kiser, and Whelpton recommend, we
have used an average of the "direct" and "indirect or residual"
methods.)[5] Clearly, the decline in the rural refined birth ratio
was by far the most important component in the total.

Table 14. Rural-Urban Components of the Decline in the White
Refined Birth Ratio: United States, 1810-1840

Absolute decline in children aged 0-4 per 1,000 women aged 20-44	Percentage distribution Decline due to:			
	Decline in rural birth ratio	*Decline in urban birth ratio*	*Rural-to- urban shift of population*	*Total*
220	78.05	10.80	11.15	100.00

Source: Calculated from Grabill, Kiser, and Whelpton, *Fertility of American Women,* table 7, p. 17.

For the year 1860 we have no information except the national white refined birth ratio, which was 886 children aged zero to four per 1,000 women aged twenty to forty-four and U.S. Bureau of the Census rural-urban proportions for the total population, white and nonwhite, which were 80.23 and 19.77 percent respectively.[6] Our first step was to estimate rural-urban proportions for the white population in 1860. Here we were assisted by a tabulation of urban places (1940 definition) generously made available to us by the Population Division of the bureau. This made it possible for us to extract from the Eighth Census of 1860 the white populations of the corresponding townships; these were then aggregated and measured as a proportion of the total white population of the United States as recorded in the census.[7] Rural-urban proportions for the white population then appeared as 78.16 and 21.84 percent.

To obtain estimates of rural and urban refined birth ratios in 1860, the obvious course was to interpolate between those for 1840 and 1910, so as to fill the gap in the series given by Grabill, Kiser, and Whelpton. Logarithmic interpolation between rural birth ratios of 1,134 in 1840 and 782 in 1910 gives a ratio of 1,020 in 1860; and similarly, interpolation between urban birth ratios of 701 in 1840 and 469 in 1910 gives a ratio of 625 in 1860.[8] But these, in conjunction with rural-urban proportions of 78.16 and 21.84 percent, yield a refined birth ratio for the country as a whole of 934. In fact, the ratio given for that year is 886; therefore, we have slightly reduced the rural and urban refined birth ratios, each in the same proportion (that is, by 5.1 percent), to levels consistent with a national figure of 886. The estimates then become 968 for the rural birth ratio and 593 for the urban.

On these assumptions, it would appear that between 1840 and 1860, 73.7 percent of the fall in the number of children aged zero to four per 1,000 white women aged twenty to forty-four was due to the decline in the rural birth ratio, 10.8 percent to the decline in the urban birth ratio, and 15.5 percent to the rural-to-urban shift of population. As we should expect, the rural component in the national decline was then a little less important than it had been between 1810 and 1840; but it was still the major component, by a very large margin. There could well be a degree of error in these estimates, since we have been forced to rely upon interpolation of rural and urban birth ratios between dates widely separated in time; it seems most unlikely, however, that the error could be so great as to have a material effect on the emphasis of the results. This comes back to the point that even in the mid-nineteenth century the urban sector was still fairly small, so that changes in urban birth ratios could hardly be expected to have formed a major component of national trends.

If this be doubted, measurement of the components of change over the whole period 1840-1910 should settle the matter. For both of these years, rural and urban refined birth ratios are given by Grabill, Kiser, and Whelpton. The national ratio fell by 461, from 1,070 in 1840 to 609 in 1910; and to this the decline in the rural birth ratio contributed 50 percent, the decline in the urban birth ratio 17 percent, and the rural-to-urban shift of population 33 percent. In the light of these figures, a rural component of a little over 70 percent in the earlier fall between 1840 and 1860 seems perfectly reasonable.

Measurement of the components of change in the white
refined birth ratio does not, in itself, explain the causal relations which may have been operating. Thus it might be
argued that urbanization was still, in some sense, the prime
mover in the national decline, because urban fertility patterns
were being "diffused" to rural areas. This theory is difficult
to assess, since its supporters do not seem to have made clear,
in an American context, the mechanism by which they suppose this diffusion to have taken place or the evidence by
which the process can be established.

Essentially, the theory of diffusion seems to rest on little
more than an assumed priority in time of a downturn in the
historical trend of urban fertility, as distinct from rural. Presumably, rural populations are supposed, with a time lag, to
have aped their fellows in the cities. It is hard to see how
the existence of a causal relation of this kind could be proved
or disproved.[9] But there is a further problem, at least in the
context of our present discussion, in that we lack evidence
to show that the trend of urban fertility did in fact turn
downward at an earlier date than the rural trend. To indicate
that this may have to be regarded as an open question, requir-
ing further investigation, we can best quote a comment made
by W. H. Bash after he had analyzed some of the data on
fertility which was gathered (but not published) in the census
of the state of New York in 1865.

Bash made a detailed study of fertility differentials by
age, nativity, occupation, and economic status in Madison
County, which he selected as being fairly representative of
upstate farming areas. Here he found that the number of
children ever born (a question in the New York census) per
100 women aged seventy-five and over in 1865 was higher
than the number ever born to women aged seventy to seventy-
four, and so progressively downward through five-year age
groups to forty-five to forty-nine, where the number of
children ever born per 100 women was 35 percent lower

than that reported by women aged seventy-five and over. Although a part of the difference in completed fertility in the five-year age groups might be attributable to a positive correlation between fertility and longevity, Bash felt this would not represent a complete explanation. There seemed rather to have been a falling trend of fertility among the successive cohorts of women born in the period from the late eighteenth century onward. These and other fertility differentials led him to conclude that "the decline in the birth rate in Madison County began very early. *And it may have begun among farm families as early as among town families.* . . . Although for the State as a whole there is a negative relationship between urbanization and industrialization and the birth rate, nevertheless, Madison County fails to fit the pattern. This is true in terms of the County's position as a unit, and it is true when one examines the differences within the County in more detail. If the diffusion of the small family pattern began in the cities in some areas of the country, then it may have come very early in the farming areas in Madison County."[10]

10

Effects of Alternative Measures on Yasuba's Thesis

This essay attempts only part of the work to be done. It is possible, for example, that a more satisfactory treatment of urbanization could be devised, to take account of any significant inverse relation there may have been between fertility and size of place—this as an alternative to the method we have used in chapters 5 and 6 of conducting an analysis simply in terms of rural child-woman ratios. Again, some consideration could perhaps be given to the likely connection between the growth of cities and the multiplication of small extraurban farms of the market-gardening kind; these would have had an effect, even if only slight, on the farm numbers we have taken as indicators of relative economic opportunities in agriculture in different states and territories.[1] Other variables, such as levels of literacy (on which there is some information at the end of the period), might be brought into the discussion. Perhaps most important of all, more attention could be given to the industrial distribution of the labor force in a state or territory, for this has the appearance in Yasuba's book of being rather more promising as an explanatory variable than the proportion of urban population (see above, pp. 7-9). Unfortunately, the data are not available for all census years in the period 1800-1860, and as Yasuba notes, "the scope and method of classification were changed from one census to another."[2] But greater use could be made of what there is.

The interesting features of American demographic experience in the first half of the nineteenth century are the high level of fertility at the beginning of the period and its gradual fall thereafter, the latter reflecting, of course, a growth of the proportion of the white population that was located in states with relatively low refined birth ratios (see table 15).

Table 15. Percentages of Total White Population in States and
Territories with Various White Refined Birth Ratios:
United States, 1800-1860

	1800	*1810*	*1820*	*1830*	*1840*	*1850*	*1860*
White refined birth ratios of:							
2,000 and over	18.1	17.0	24.7	21.4	13.9	0.1	0.2
1,500-1,999	70.7	69.4	58.2	36.2	36.7	39.4	29.6
1,000-1,499	11.2	13.6	17.1	42.4	43.5	51.2	62.0
Less than 1,000					5.9	9.3	8.2
Total	100.0	100.0	100.0	100.0	100.0	100.0	100.0

Note: White refined birth ratios are the number of children aged 0-9
per 1,000 white women aged 16-44. Standardized ratios are used from
1830 onward. Total population is that for states and territories for
which Yasuba gives refined birth ratios. In all years this represents more
than 99 percent of the total white population of the United States.
Source: Calculated from Yasuba, *Birth Rates,* tables 2.7 and 4.12, pp.
61-62 and 131-32; and U.S. censuses, 1800-1860.

Our object has been to assess the influence likely to have
been exerted by two factors: the diminishing availability of
easily accessible land, and increasing urbanization.

We began with cross-section analyses based on nonpara-
metric methods very similar to Yasuba's own. There were
two differences. First, in place of population density per
1,000 acres of arable land (the latter being defined as cropland as of 1949) used by Yasuba in his rank correlations, we
calculated the ratio of the number of adults in a state or
territory at a given date to the number of farms enumerated
there at a later date (1850, 1860, or 1880). The adult-farm
ratio was intended, in effect, as an inverse index of opportunities for additional agricultural settlement. Second, as an
alternative to Yasuba's method of "moving standardization,"
we computed Kendall's coefficient of partial rank correlation between the white refined birth ratio of a state or ter-

ritory, the adult-farm ratio, and the proportion of urban population. On the whole, results were consistent with Yasuba's in that markedly higher partial coefficients between the birth ratio and the adult-farm ratio were obtained for cross sections in the period 1800-1840 than between the birth ratio and the urban proportion. In 1850 and 1860 the former weakened and the latter became stronger, although even at these dates the adult-farm ratio still appeared to be the more important variable.

Because Kendall's coefficient of partial rank correlation cannot be tested for significance, we then computed, for each cross section, a multiple regression of the white refined birth ratio of a state or territory on the logarithms of the adult-farm ratio and the urban proportion. (Logarithmic transformation was adopted on the ground that the relations postulated in the regression seemed likely to be curvilinear rather than linear.) For each cross section, the coefficient of partial linear correlation between the birth ratio and the logarithm of the adult-farm ratio suggested a very close inverse association, significant at the 1 percent level (though with a slight weakening at the end of the period); that between the birth ratio and the logarithm of the urban proportion was never significantly different from zero, even at the 5 percent level. The proportion of urban population appeared to be of little value as an explanatory variable.

At this stage we were concerned about two aspects of the analysis. It seemed unsatisfactory simply to use the proportion of urban population in a state or territory as an explanatory variable, because this took no account of interstate differences in the distribution of urban inhabitants between towns and cities of various sizes. Urban fertility might well have tended to be related inversely with size of place, so that a given urban proportion should have counted more heavily if those of whom it was composed were concentrated in a few large towns rather than dispersed in many small ones, perhaps only marginally distinguished in their attitudes and economic and social conditions from the surrounding rural populations. As an alternative, therefore, we calculated a rural white refined birth ratio for each state or territory at census dates in the period 1800-1840 (after which the method ceases to be practicable) and used Kendall's coefficient of rank correlation to measure the association in each cross section with an adult-farm ratio in which the numerator consisted of rural adults only. This precluded comparisons of the partial association between the birth ratio and density of agricultural settlement and the birth ratio and urbanization; but in isolating the first relation it had the compensating advantage of being less open to possible statistical bias, especially of the kind that can affect the results of multiple regression analysis in cases (such as the present one) where the two explanatory variables are themselves correlated moderately, and sometimes closely, in a cross section.[3] We found close inverse associations between the rural birth ratio of a state or territory and the ratio of rural adults to the number of farms enumerated in 1860 or 1880. Kendall's coefficient of rank correlation was of the order of -.7 to -.8 at all five census dates 1800-1840 and was significant throughout at the 1 percent level.

Our other major misgiving arose from the very strength of the associations we had obtained between the refined birth ratio and density of agricultural settlement (or as the inverse of the latter variable, economic opportunity for the creation of new rural households). This doubt was further intensified when we found that the association emerged with almost equal strength in two cross-section analyses conducted for counties within the state of New York. It seemed possible that the associations were being bolstered by some more purely demographic factor having its greatest influence in frontier regions in the early stage of their settlement. This factor, we suggested, might have been connected with a characteristic of internal migration to formerly unoccupied areas. If internal migration was selective of married women rather than single, it could have raised the proportion of wives among all women aged sixteen to forty-four initially to very high levels, from whence it could later have been expected to decline. In circumstances of this kind, the availability of unoccupied land, by its effect in attracting new settlers, would still be relevant to explain interstate or intercounty fertility differentials at a given time, or at least to assist in doing so. But it might not be relevant to explain trends over time in the national white refined birth ratio— unless, of course, a more basic socioeconomic relation between fertility and opportunities for additional agricultural settlement "not far from the place of residence" of the older-established communities could be discerned beneath the demographic influences arising from internal migration and helping to widen interstate fertility differentials.

To test a hypothesis that such a socioeconomic relation did exist, we limited our analysis to older states having adult-farm ratios at a level of median or above in each cross section. These would have been much less affected by the entry of migrants from elsewhere in the United States (though toward the end of the period some consideration might have to be given to the effect of intakes of newcomers from overseas). The inverse associations between the refined birth ratio and the adult-farm ratio were noticeably weakened at the beginning of the period (in cross sections for 1800 and 1810), but the effect thereafter was not so pronounced. We attach particular importance to the association between the rural white refined birth ratio of a state included in these more confined cross sections and the (rural) adult-farm ratio in 1820, 1830, and 1840, as shown by Kendall's coefficient of rank correlation. Multiple regression analyses, relating to the refined birth ratios of total state populations, both urban and rural, and introducing the proportion of urban population

as a second explanatory variable, gave results consistent
with the hypothesis that, in older-settled areas, fertility
varied inversely with the adult-farm ratio (or directly with
the availability of easily accessible land); and we were able
to extend the impression of a significant partial association
to cross sections for the birth ratios of 1850 and 1860.[4]
On the other hand, the proportion of urban population in
a state appeared to be of little use as an explanatory variable. As a further step, we added the logarithm of the sex
ratio to our multiple regressions, intending it as a variable
to take account of demographic effects that might have
been produced by out-migration from the older states.
This addition made little difference to results except at
the beginning of the period, and particularly to those for
the cross section relating to the birth ratios of 1810.

Finally, for more densely settled states, there appeared
to be a significant association between the increase over
time of the adult-farm ratio and the decrease of the white
refined birth ratio. This was particularly evident for change
over the first half of the period as measured in eight states
with adult-farm ratios at a level of median or above in the
cross section for 1800. In the second half of the period,
using states with adult-farm ratios at a level of median or
above in the cross section for 1830, we found a clear weakening of the association—as Yasuba had detected by different
means in his own work.[5] However, when adult-farm ratios
were based on farm numbers in 1880 (but not when we
used farm numbers in 1860), the partial association between
the increase of the logarithm of the adult-farm ratio and
the decrease of the birth ratio, though weaker, was still significant at the 5 percent level.

An unresolved problem is to account for the loosening of
the partial association between the increase of the adult-
farm ratio and the decrease of the standardized refined birth
ratio in the latter part of the period 1800-1860. International

migration may have played some part in this, but probably other factors, yet to be identified, were involved. For example, improved transport facilities tending to reduce the frictions formerly affecting internal migration might need to be considered. Again, it may be that a growing proportion of those officially classified as "rural" were becoming less influenced in their family-building behavior by economic opportunities in agriculture. As an extreme case, it is sobering to recall the state of Vermont, whose urban proportion was only 2 percent in 1850 but which had 48 percent of its white males over fifteen years of age employed in nonagricultural pursuits.[6] As we have already said, it seems clear that in any further work, greater attention ought to be given to changes in the industrial distribution of the labor force.

Nevertheless, in spite of the loose ends, we feel we have done enough to be impressed by the force of Yasuba's thesis, which has shown up well on the alternative measures we have applied. We have suggested some qualifications to his argument, but the main outlines of his work stand unaffected. There does seem to have been a meaningful socioeconomic relation between the refined birth ratio and the abundance or scarcity of opportunities near to the place of residence for the establishment of new farms, and this may help to account both for the height of American fertility at the beginning of the nineteenth century and its subsequent downward trend. In this period, and particularly toward its end, levels of fertility may also have been influenced by the progress of urbanization, but like Yasuba, we cannot accept the hypothesis that this was a dominating force before 1860. Indeed, the general effect of our analysis, if anything, has been to weaken rather than strengthen the claims of this factor. Moreover, whatever may have been true at other times or in other places, our impression is that urbanization was not a necessary condition for a reduction of fertility in the United States in the first half of the nineteenth century.

Notes

INTRODUCTION

1. A. J. Coale and Melvin Zelnik, *New Estimates of Fertility and Population in the United States* (Princeton: Princeton University Press, 1963), p. 35.
2. Baltimore: The Johns Hopkins Press, 1962.
3. Irene B. Taeuber, *Journal of Economic History* 23 (1963): 260-61.
4. Yasuba, *Birth Rates*, p. 187.
5. "The Growth of Population in America, 1700-1860," in *Population in History*, ed. D. V. Glass and D. E. C. Eversley (London: Edward Arnold, 1965), p. 677.

CHAPTER 1

1. Yasuba notes that others have given slightly different measures (pp. 23-37). For example, W. S. Thompson and P. K. Whelpton in their *Population Trends in the United States* (New York: McGraw-Hill, 1933) used the number of children aged 0-4, not 0-9 as does Yasuba. This raises some problems of estimation, since the censuses of 1800, 1810, and 1820 did not enumerate separately children aged 0-4.
2. The basic measure taken from the Thirteenth Census is "the age-specific ratio of 'own' children under 5 to native white women in the United States in 1910," which is adjusted to give estimates of age-specific ratios of children under 10 (Yasuba, *Birth Rates*, pp. 129-30). For the method of standardization, see also pp. 30-31 and p. 132, table 4.12, note *a*.
3. Ibid., pp. 130-34. Yasuba discusses some other ways in which the refined birth ratio could give biased impressions of levels and trends of fertility (pp. 34-37). For example, had the necessary information been available, it would have been desirable to take account of changes in child mortality, which would have affected the numbers surviving at census times. Again, it is possible that children aged 0-9 were more likely to be underenumerated in a census than women of childbearing age. If the percentage undercount of children relative to that of women was constant, the usefulness of the refined birth ratio as a measure of *changes* in fertility would not be affected, but the facts could well have been otherwise. Summing up, he thinks it unlikely that factors other than fertility could account for "a major part" of the decline in the refined birth ratio—this on the ground that they probably operated in different direc-

101

tions, with little net effect (p. 49). Here it is worth noting that painstaking estimates of the total fertility rate in the United States made recently by Coale and Zelnik suggest that it fell by 26 percent between 1800 and 1860 (*New Estimates of Fertility*, p. 36). This can be compared with the 29 percent fall in the unstandardized refined birth ratio given by Yasuba. Taking the period 1830-60, the fall in the total fertility rate as estimated by Coale and Zelnik is 20.5 percent, while that for Yasuba's standardized refined birth ratio is 20.1 percent.

4. We have not included the Mountain and Pacific divisions in the graphs. For these the data do not extend back before 1850.

5. We agree with Yasuba in thinking that the possibility of limitation of intramarital fertility as a factor influencing refined birth ratios should not be dismissed lightly, even in this early period. There is some evidence to suggest that it existed in parts of western Europe in the eighteenth century and perhaps even the later seventeenth. On this see J. T. Krause, "Some Implications of Recent Work in Historical Demography," *Comparative Studies in Society and History* 1 (1958-59): 184-87; E. A. Wrigley, "Family Limitation in Pre-Industrial England," *Economic History Review*, 2d ser. 19 (1966): 82-109.

6. Yasuba, *Birth Rates*, p. 159.

7. Ibid., p. 168. Yasuba also analyzes the association between the *change* in the refined birth ratio of a state or territory and the *change* in population density, using a method which he describes as "standardized rank correlation" (pp. 166-68). This would take considerable space to explain and the reader seeking further information is referred to pp. 149 ff. of the book. Here it is sufficient to note that Yasuba believes the hypothesis relating to the importance of the availability of easily accessible land as a determinant of fertility is supported also by "a close association between the change in population density and the change in the refined birth ratio during the first half of the period," though the association became weaker after 1830 (pp. 168-69).

8. Ibid., p. 158. This conclusion is derived partly from an analysis of the association between the *change* in the refined birth ratio of a state or territory and *change* in the proportion of urban population, again using "standardized rank correlation." Here Yasuba compares his results with those referred to in note 7 to this chapter.

9. Yasuba, *Birth Rates*, pp. 162-63.

10. Ibid., p. 175.

CHAPTER 2

1. These are Rhode Island, 43.8%; Massachusetts, 37.9%; Louisiana, 29.9%; Maryland, 24.2%; New York, 19.4%; and Pennsylvania, 17.9% (U.S. Bureau of the Census 1940 urban-rural definition).
2. Yasuba notes that the change in the direction of greater urbanization (and industrialization) was "very gradual until around 1840 and then suddenly became accelerated" (*Birth Rates*, p. 142).
3. See M. G. Kendall, "Partial Rank Correlation," *Biometrika* 32 (1941-42): 277-83, esp. p. 283; also his *Rank Correlation Methods*, 3d ed. (London: Charles Griffin, 1962), pp. 117-22.
4. The words *filling up* were suggested by the *Report* of the Superintendent of the Seventh Census of 1850 who, when discussing the internal movement of population, said: "When the fertile plains of the West shall have been filled up, and men of scanty means cannot by a mere change of location acquire a homestead, the inhabitants of each State will become comparatively stationary, and our countrymen will exhibit that attachment to the homes of their childhood, the want of which is sometimes cited as an unfavorable trait in our national character." *Report of the Superintendent of the Census for December 1, 1852; to Which is Appended the Report for December 1, 1851* (Washington: House of Representatives, 1853), p. 15. Again, the Superintendent is quoted as saying in his *Preliminary Report* on the Eighth Census of 1860: "The old agricultural States may be said to be filled up, so far as regards the resources adapted to a rural population in the present condition of agricultural science." See U.S. Civil War Centennial Commission, *The United States on the Eve of the Civil War* (Washington: 1963), p. 2.
5. *Report for December 1, 1852*, p. 15.
6. See Yasuba, *Birth Rates*, tables 2.7, 4.12, and 5.3, pp. 61-62, 131-32, and 143-44.
7. *Migration from Vermont* (Montpelier: Vermont Historical Society, 1948).
8. Ibid., p. 77. Another writer, R. A. Billington, notes that "overcrowding" in older New England states had raised land prices there to such an extent that by the 1790s "even moderately good farms sold for from $14 to $50 an acre. Younger sons—and they were plentiful in prolific New England families—refused to pay such prices for rock-strewn hillsides when they could buy fertile lands in the West for $2 or $3 an acre." He also says: "Those same con-

ditions—overcrowding, high prices, exorbitant taxes, and con-
servatism—also existed in the Middle States and South, but other
factors in both those sections helped speed the exodus." See
Westward Expansion (New York: Macmillan, 1949), p. 247.

9. Stilwell, *Migration from Vermont,* pp. 96-97; see also p. 66. Stilwell gives an estimate of 7,000 for the population in 1771 (p. 79),
while the census figure for 1810 is 218,000. The average annual
rate of growth between these dates works out at 9.2 percent.

10. Ibid., p. 108.

11. Ibid., pp. 117-24.

12. Ibid., pp. 125-30, 137. Blows to Vermont listed by Stilwell include the embargo of 1808, flood in 1811, the Vermont State
Bank collapse of 1811-12, the War of 1812, disease in 1813, and
the "cold season" of 1816.

13. Ibid., pp. 157-59, 172-73, 211.

14. The average annual rate of growth of Vermont's population between 1810 and 1850 was about 0.9 percent, or one-tenth of that
in the preceding forty-year period.

15. *Migration from Vermont,* pp. 236-37.

16. N. A. McNall, *An Agricultural History of the Genesee Valley,
1790-1860* (Philadelphia: University of Pennsylvania Press, 1952),
p. 68.

17. McNall's population of 23,148 in 1810 grew to 246,232 in 1860
(ibid., p. 66, note). It was 200,604 in 1840 (*Compendium of the
Sixth Census*). The average annual rate of growth is about 7.5 percent in the period 1810-40 compared with just over 1 percent in
the period 1840-60.

18. McNall, *Agricultural History of the Genesee Valley,* p. 232.

19. Ibid., pp. 243-44.

20. A. G. Smith, *Economic Readjustment of an Old Cotton State:
South Carolina, 1820-1860* (Columbia: University of South
Carolina Press, 1958). Reference to Yasuba's table, reprinted as
table A above, shows that in most cross sections, the inverse
association between population density per 1,000 acres of arable
land and the white refined birth ratio was closer for free states
and territories than for slave states and territories.

21. Ibid., pp. 23, 29, 34.

22. Ibid., pp. 25-26, 29-30.

23. Ibid., p. 33.

24. Ibid., pp. 33-34. Yasuba notes: "Even in the eastern seaboard areas
[of the United States] the extent of land-use was more limited

than in western Europe" (*Birth Rates,* p. 159).

25. "Standardized" is important, because the works we have been considering, especially Stilwell's, serve to remind us of the high proportion of internal migrants likely to have been in the young adult age groups (under 30 years). It is indeed unfortunate that Yasuba was not able to standardize his refined birth ratios for differences of age distribution within the childbearing period except for census dates from 1830 onward. Though its effect was "minor in most instances" between 1830 and 1860 (see above, p. 3), it would be comforting to be sure that this conclusion could be applied also to the period 1800-1820.

26. Elizabeth W. Gilboy and E. M. Hoover mention several possible causes of the decline in fertility. One is that "good unoccupied farm land became less immediately accessible to the bulk of the population as the frontier edged westward; an increasing proportion of the population lived in more fully settled areas where the establishment of a source of livelihood for a new family was perhaps less a matter of following the beaten path. More of an economic premium was set on occupational mobility." See "Population and Immigration," in *American Economic History*, ed. S. E. Harris (New York: McGraw-Hill, 1961), p. 250. Occupational mobility would have been an alternative, of course, to geographical mobility, but it too may have been subject to frictions.

27. See J. Hajnal, "European Marriage Patterns in Perspective," in *Population in History,* ed. Glass and Eversley, p. 101. Conrad and Irene B. Taeuber have said: "In the late eighteenth and early nineteenth centuries, as in the colonial period, marriage must have been almost universal and it must have occurred at early ages. . . . marriage in the middle teens must have been prevalent in the rural population which comprised a large portion of the national total in the early period." *The Changing Population of the United States* (New York: John Wiley, 1958), p. 148.

CHAPTER 3

1. Reasons for our adoption of this second criterion are discussed in more detail below, pp. 31-33.

2. Data of farm numbers by state or territory for the period 1850-1910, together with intercensal percentage increases, were set out conveniently in the *Thirteenth Census (1910)*, vol. 5, Agriculture (Washington: Government Printing Office, 1913), pp. 68-72. There

is a survey also of the definitions of "farms" used in earlier censuses. In summary, the census of 1850 called for returns of all farms whose annual produce amounted to $100 in value. It was not intended to include small lots, owned or worked by persons following other pursuits, whose produce was of less than $100 in value. In 1860, no instructions on this subject were given to the enumerators. A much more elaborate definition was used in 1880. Farms were to be understood to include "all considerable nurseries, orchards, and market gardens . . . Mere cabbage and potato patches, family vegetable gardens, and ornamental lawns . . . will be excluded. No farm will be reported of less than 3 acres unless $500 worth of produce has been actually sold off from it during the year. . . . A farm is what is owned or leased by one man and cultivated under his care. A distant wood or sheep pasture . . . is to be treated as a part of the farm; but whereever there is a resident overseer, or a manager, there a farm is to be reported." See also above p. 94.

3. *Report on the Productions of Agriculture as Returned at the Tenth Census (June 1, 1880)* (Washington: Government Printing Office, 1883), p. x.

4. There is a slight discontinuity in that for the period 1790-1820 "adults" have been taken as those aged 16 and over, whereas for 1830-50 it was easier to take numbers aged 15 and over, corresponding to the census classification then in use. In cross-section analysis, this is not important.

5. Two errors in Yasuba's data of white refined birth ratios that affect the ranking of states and territories have been corrected. The ratio given in his table 2.7 (p. 61) for Virginia in 1800 is 1,954; it should be 1,824. The standardized ratio given in his table 4.12 (p. 131) for Kentucky in 1840 is 1,987; it should be 1,897.

6. Standardized refined birth ratios are used from 1830 onward. As in the case of correlations between birth ratios and adult-farm ratios, a time lag has been adopted by which the birth ratio in a given year is related to the urban proportion at a date ten years earlier.

CHAPTER 4

1. Examples of observations where there were marked departures from linearity are provided by the birth ratios of Kentucky and Tennessee in 1800, Indiana in 1820, and Illinois in 1830. These

cannot be explained by reference to urbanization, since the proportion of urban population is recorded as zero in each case.

2. An obvious example would be Vermont (discussed above, pp. 14 - 15), whose proportion of urban population is recorded as zero in the period 1800-1840 and which had risen only to 2 percent by 1860. This state always stood out by itself from the main body of the scatters. But there were others of the same kind. (To plot observations for states and territories whose urban proportions were zero, thus having no logarithm, it was necessary to assign to them arbitrarily a tiny percentage of urban inhabitants.)

3. The figure chosen is of little importance. Results shown in tables 3 and 4, below, have been recomputed for an arbitrary value of 0.1 percent instead of 0.5 percent. The differences were negligible.

4. See, for example, Gustaf Utterström, "Two Essays on Population in Eighteenth-Century Scandinavia," in *Population in History,* ed. Glass and Eversley, pp. 523-48, esp. p. 528, where Utterström says: "No investigation has been made of the extent to which fertility variations were related to age differences in women at marriage and/or to voluntary birth control, but both factors obviously played a role. High marital fertility and birth rates evidently existed in areas where opportunities for internal colonization were good, such as Finland and some Swedish (and probably Norwegian) woodlands. Low fertility and birth rates occurred in old, cultivated plains areas where tenant farmers made up a relatively large part of the population; Denmark is the outstanding example."

CHAPTER 5

1. We are indebted to the Population Division of the bureau for a tabulation of urban places in 1840, 1850, and 1860, together with numbers of their populations.

2. In this census, numbers of white women aged 20-39 can be obtained directly by addition of two ten-year age groups, but those aged 16-19 and 40-44 must be derived as estimates. They were interpolated by means of formulas adopted by Yasuba, *Birth Rates,* pp. 32-34.

3. On this method, see above, pp. 3-4; also Yasuba, *Birth Rates,* pp. 128-30, and table 5.12, pp. 131-32, note *a.*

4. Linear correlation was used in preference to rank correlation to save time in computing, for which a programmed desk calculator

was available. Populations of urban places were rounded to the
nearest hundred.

5. Urban places (1940 definition) of the period 1800-1840 are
identified by G. R. Taylor in "American Urban Growth Preceding the Railway Age," *Journal of Economic History* 27 (1967):
pp. 309-39. On advice kindly supplied by the Population Division,
U.S. Bureau of the Census, we have subtracted the populations of
a few urban places not listed by Taylor for 1840. These are Cambridge, Charlestown, Dorchester, and Roxbury in Massachusetts;
Brooklyn in New York; and Kensington, Moyamensing, Northern
Liberties, Southwark, and Spring Garden in Pennsylvania. In nearly all cases we have been able to subtract the populations of townships identified as urban places under the 1940 definition, but in
some instances we found it necessary to use the county as a unit,
thereby removing small numbers of rural inhabitants who rightly
should have been left where they were. The distortion would be
negligible.

   We should have liked to repeat the calculations for the years
1850 and 1860. However, the Seventh and Eighth Censuses, unlike earlier ones, did not give age distributions for townships.
The next best thing would have been to subtract the populations
of counties containing urban places, but this would have resulted
in a considerable loss of data, especially in the older-settled areas.
Results would not have been comparable with those for earlier
years.

6. In cases where counties containing urban places had been removed
instead of townships, an adjustment was made to farm numbers
recorded for the state or territory in question before calculation
of an adult-farm ratio.

CHAPTER 6

1. Women and children in the relevant age groups enumerated in
townships classified as urban places have been subtracted from
eastern and western area totals for the period 1800-1840. For the
years 1850 and 1860, in which age distributions of the populations
of townships are not available, a more clumsy procedure has had
to be adopted: we have made subtractions covering whole counties
containing urban places. (Corresponding adjustments were made
to the numbers of farms used as denominators in calculating adult-
farm ratios for these years.) Fortunately, the level of urbanization

in Virginia was not high, even in the eastern area, and not many
counties were affected.

2. We are grateful to the New York Historical Society for a map
   showing county boundaries in 1810. This we have modified to
   take account of new counties formed between 1810 and 1820,
   as listed in *Census of the State of New York, for 1855* (Albany:
   1857), intro., p. xxxiii. Since we have been unable to obtain a
   map showing exact county boundaries in 1820, those we have
   used should be regarded as approximate only. We are confident,
   however, that the broad pattern of birth ratios has not been mis-
   represented.

3. As in the preceding section, the variables now being correlated
   have not been separated by a ten-year interval.

4. Similar results were derived from an earlier, alternative calculation based simply on the white refined birth ratios of counties,
   without adjustment to remove the urban components. From
   this we dropped not only the county of New York but also seven
   other southeastern counties that had the highest adult-farm ratios
   in the state (in descending order, Kings, Richmond, Columbia,
   Dutchess, Albany, Westchester, and Rensselaer). Kendall's coefficient of rank correlation between the refined birth ratios of
   the remaining 37 areas and adult-farm ratios was −.62, significant
   at the 1 percent level.

5. The method is referred to above, pp. 3-4; see also Yasuba, *Birth
   Rates,* pp. 128-30, and table 4.12, pp. 131-32, note *a*.

CHAPTER 7

1. By 1845, proportions in the former group of counties had fallen
   to levels of 61-65 percent, while those in the latter group remained
   much the same, within limits of 52-57 percent.

2. *Migration from Vermont,* pp. 140, 143.

3. See note 8 to chapter 2, above. It will be seen that if we allowed
   for the possibility of change in the industrial distribution of the
   labor force and rising urbanization in Vermont, the decline of
   fertility could be expected to be reinforced.

4. Yasuba based his conclusions partly upon an analysis of this kind,
   applying it to all states and territories, new as well as old, that
   were included in the initial cross sections for two thirty-year sub-
   periods and using change in "population density" rather than the
   adult-farm ratio. See above, note 7 to chapter 1.

5. This proposition makes no allowance for the possible effects on fertility of increasing urbanization, which could well have gone ahead (though perhaps more slowly) even if there had been no pressure of numbers on agricultural land available in more densely settled eastern states.

6. As in chapter 6, table 7, the variables being correlated have not been separated by a ten-year interval.

7. This still occurs if the regressions are recomputed without logarithmic transformation of the two explanatory variables. In this case, using adult-farm ratios based on farm numbers in 1880, the seven coefficients of partial linear correlation between the refined birth ratio of a state and the adult-farm ratio become $-.75$, $-.64$, $-.87**$, $-.87**$, $-.85**$, $-.64*$, and $-.68**$, while those between the refined birth ratio and the proportion of urban population become $.39$, $-.10$, $.40$, $.35$, $.22$, $-.10$, and $.33$.

8. Sex ratios are shown by Yasuba, *Birth Rates*, table 4.11, pp. 127-28.

9. Ibid., pp. 125-27. T'ien's paper on "A Demographic Aspect of Interstate Variations in American Fertility, 1800-1860" appeared in *The Milbank Memorial Fund Quarterly* 37 (1959): 49-59.

10. T'ien, "A Demographic Aspect of Interstate Variations in American Fertility," p. 57.

11. Ibid., pp. 54-55.

12. Other states included with urban proportions of less than 10 percent are Indiana (4.5%), Virginia (7.1%), and Kentucky (7.5%).

13. Yasuba, *Birth Rates*, p. 145.

14. As shown above (p. 106n4), there is a minor discontinuity in that for the year 1800 "adults" are taken as those aged 16 and over, whereas for 1840 we used numbers aged 15 and over, according to the current census classification. We are assuming, in effect, that changes in the adult-farm ratios of all states would have been affected to about the same extent by the discontinuity.

   It should be noted also that in measuring the absolute decrease in the rural white refined birth ratio of a state between 1800 and 1840, we are comparing an unstandardized birth ratio in 1800 with a standardized ratio in 1840. The only possible way of assessing the likely importance of this discontinuity is to recompute the regressions using unstandardized birth ratios both in 1800 and 1840. In this case, when (rural) adult-farm ratios are based on farm numbers in 1860, the correlation coefficient is .73; with adult-farm ratios based on farm numbers in 1880, it is .75.

15. If sex ratios were not included in the regression, the partial correlation coefficient between the absolute change of the birth ratio of a state and the change of the logarithm of the adult-farm ratio would become −.88, significant at the 1 percent level, and that between the change of the birth ratio and the change of the logarithm of the urban proportion would become −.16.

16. It is proper to recall that, although the refined birth ratios of 1830 and later have been standardized for differences in the age distribution of women within the childbearing span, those for 1800, 1810, and 1820 cannot be treated in this way. For each state, therefore, we are measuring the difference between an unstandardized refined birth ratio in 1800 and a standardized ratio in 1840. We have to hope that the effects of standardization would have been "minor in most instances" before 1830, as Yasuba found them to be later, from 1830 onward.

17. An exception is noted in table 12, above.

18. If we use adult-farm ratios based on farm numbers in 1860 instead of 1880, Virginia displaces Vermont as a state with an adult-farm ratio at a level of median or above in 1800. The partial correlation coefficients between the absolute change of the birth ratio and change of the logarithms of the adult-farm ratio, urban proportion, and sex ratio then become −.86 (significant at the 5 percent level), −.59, and −.69 respectively.

19. Much the same change in the coefficients occurs if we substitute Virginia for Vermont and repeat the analysis using adult-farm ratios based on farm numbers in 1860.

20. *Birth Rates,* p. 166.

21. With adult-farm ratios based on farm numbers in 1860, states to be added are New York, Pennsylvania, South Carolina, and Vermont.

22. If sex ratios are not included in the regression, the partial correlation coefficient between the absolute change of the birth ratio and change of the logarithm of the adult-farm ratio remains much the same at −.70, significant at the 5 percent level, while that between change of the birth ratio and change of the logarithm of the urban proportion becomes −.25.

23. Results are not nearly so good, however, when adult-farm ratios are based on farm numbers in 1860. Here the three partial coefficients are −.31, +.18, and +.03 respectively, and the square of the coefficient of multiple correlation is only .170.

CHAPTER 8

1. See U.S. Bureau of the Census, *Historical Statistics of the United States, Colonial Times to 1957* (Washington, D.C.: 1960), p. 57 (for total immigrants), and p. 7 (for estimated population).
2. *Birth Rates*, p. 184.
3. United Nations, *The Determinants and Consequences of Population Trends* (New York: United Nations, 1953), p. 139.
4. See A. Ross Eckler and Jack Zlotnick, "Immigration and the Labor Force," *Annals of the American Academy of Political and Social Science* 262 (March 1949): 92-101, and authorities cited.
5. *New Estimates of Fertility*, esp. chapter 4, "Long-Term Fertility Trends in the United States Compared to Those in Selected European Countries" (pp. 32-41).
6. In addition to the graphs shown by Coale and Zelnick, see the figures for crude birth rates of various European countries in the periods 1841-50 and 1851-60 given by D. V. Glass, "World Population, 1800-1950," in H. J. Habakkuk and M. Postan, eds., *The Cambridge Economic History of Europe, vol. 6, The Industrial Revolutions and After* (Cambridge: The University Press, 1965), Pt. 1, pp. 68-69; also H. W. Methorst, "Survey of Birth-Rates of the World," *The Eugenics Review* 19 (1927-28): 116-27.
7. Graphs showing regional birth rates in Germany during the second half of the nineteenth century are given by W. G. Hoffmann, "The Take-Off in Germany," in W. W. Rostow, ed., *The Economics of Take-Off into Sustained Growth* (London: Macmillan, 1963), p. 98.
8. *The Population of Ireland 1750-1845* (Oxford: The Clarendon Press, 1950), p. 30.
9. K. H. Connell, "Some Unsettled Problems in English and Irish Population History, 1750-1845," *Irish Historical Studies* 7 (1951): 228, note 3.
10. "Marriage and Population Growth in Ireland, 1750-1845," *The Economic History Review*, 2d ser. 16 (1963): 307-9. Drake also compares Ireland and Norway, concluding that "there was little difference in fertility."
11. "Census of Ireland, 1841, Reports of the Commissioners," *Parliamentary Papers* 24 (1843): xl. It should be noted that although the commissioners reported a number of "births" for each year during the period 1832-41, these were not derived directly from a question asked in the census. In the commissioners' words, they

were "constructed simply by adding the numbers now alive at every year of age, for the last 10 years, to the numbers whose ages at death [about which a question was asked] show them to have been born in the same year" (ibid., p. xl). Deficiencies of this procedure have been discussed in G. S. L. Tucker, "Irish Fertility Ratios before the Famine," *Economic History Review* 23 (August 1970): 267-84.

12. "Census of Ireland, 1841," pp. 488-89.

13. The existence of the second of the three categories we have listed is suggested by minor peaks shown at ages "one month," "three months," "six months," and "nine months." Presumably there would have been another at "twelve months" even if some aged one and less than two years had not been included in the group as well.

14. There is no evidence of this in statistics of deaths at the relevant ages reported in the census.

15. Calculated from B. R. Mitchell, *Abstract of British Historical Statistics* (Cambridge: The University Press, 1962), pp. 12-14.

16. Quoted by Yasuba, *Birth Rates,* table 1.2, p. 27.

17. *Report of the Superintendent of the Census for December 1, 1852; to Which is Appended the Report for December 1, 1851,* pp. 118-19.

18. The Superintendent uses the words "indiscriminately taken," but it would be interesting to know what methods were used.

19. *Population of the United States in 1860; Compiled from the Original Returns of the Eighth Census* (Washington, D.C.: 1864), intro., pp. xviii ff.

20. Calculated from U.S. Bureau of the Census, *Historical Statistics of the United States,* Series C 133 and 138, p. 62.

21. See Yasuba, *Birth Rates,* p. 130, note 43.

22. Here standardization cannot be carried out exactly, since we are dealing with women aged 15-40, not 15-39 as for the women entering over the period 1820-60.

23. The native-American ratio, of course, has not been standardized. But this would have affected it only a little either way.

24. It is worth noting, however, that the difference between American birth ratios and those of immigrants on arrival can still be found in years before the rotten potatoes of the later 1840s and the diseases that affected the Irish and Germans at about the same time. For example, we can take the year 1840. In *Historical Statistics of the United States,* Series C 133-38 (p. 62) give total im-

migrants, percent male, and numbers in the broad age groups under 15 years, 15 to 40 years, and over 40. From these it is possible to estimate the number of immigrant children aged 0-14 per 1,000 immigrant women aged 15-40. To derive this figure, we have made two assumptions. First, that immigrant children aged 0-14 were divided between male and female in the same proportions as the aggregate of children aged 0-14 entering the United States in the period 1820-60, for which statistics were given in the Eighth Census. (These proportions were 52.8 percent male and 47.2 percent female.) By subtraction, this allows us to obtain the number of immigrant women aged over 14. Second, that of these, the proportion aged 15-39 was the same as that among the aggregate of women aged over 14 entering in the period 1820-60 (86.9 percent). For the year 1840 we can calculate in this way a ratio of 1,107 children aged 0-14 per 1,000 immigrant women aged 15-39. The corresponding ratio for the white population of the United States in that year, native and foreign-born, was 2,195.

25. This might have applied also to internal migration and could account for the stability or rising tendencies of refined birth ratios evident in some new territories in the very early years of settlement.

26. Yasuba apparently accepts a view that immigrant fertility was higher than native American even in the period before 1860, though "probably . . . not so much higher than native fertility as in later years" (*Birth Rates*, p. 184). If this were so, we could expect the standardized refined birth ratio of a given cohort of immigrant women, given time, to have risen above the native American.

27. Of total arrivals over the period 1820-60, for whom a distribution by age and sex was given in the Eighth Census (see above, pp. 76-77), 63 percent of those aged 15 and over were male.

28. Ratios of the foreign-born to total white population by state or territory in 1860 are given by Yasuba, *Birth Rates*, table 5.17, p. 182. The range is from 0.5% in North Carolina to 68.9% in Dakota, or if the latter is excluded on the ground that its total population was very small, to 45.3% in California, 35.8% in Wisconsin, and 34.7% in Minnesota. In 1850 the Seventh Census shows similar ratios for Wisconsin and Minnesota but a much lower one for California.

29. This is suggested by statistics of differential immigrant fertility

extracted by W. H. Bash from information obtained in the census of the state of New York in 1865; see "Differential Fertility in Madison County, New York, 1865," *The Milbank Memorial Fund Quarterly* 33 (1955): 161-86, esp. pp. 165-71.

30. See Yasuba, *Birth Rates,* tables 2.7 and 4.12, pp. 61 and 131.

31. Ibid., p. 187.

CHAPTER 9

1. See the passage from Yasuba quoted by Potter in "The Growth of Population in America, 1700-1860," p. 677, note 8.

2. Ibid., p. 678.

3. Ibid., p. 673 and note 84. The states for which Potter gives separate county, city, or district figures are Connecticut, New York, Pennsylvania, Virginia, Ohio, and Louisiana.

4. W. H. Grabill, C. V. Kiser, and P. K. Whelpton, *The Fertility of American Women* (New York: John Wiley, 1958), pp. 16-19.

5. Ibid., p. 17, note 13.

6. U.S. Bureau of the Census, *Historical Statistics of the United States,* pp. 14 and 24.

7. In the Eighth Census we were unable to identify nine urban places out of the total 392 in the bureau's tabulation. However, the tabulation had included their populations. These were all small, and we classified them as white and nonwhite by applying weighted averages of the proportions for other urban places in the states in question.

8. We have used logarithmic interpolation in preference to simple arithmetic interpolation because it yields rural and urban refined birth ratios in 1860 more nearly consistent with the known national ratio of 886 in that year.

9. It is possible, of course, that urban fertility from very early times had been at a generally lower level than rural fertility. But to accept this would be different from assuming that rural fertility began to decline, whenever that may have been, *because* of a prior example set by city dwellers.

10. "Differential Fertility in Madison County, New York, 1865," pp. 168-69, 186 (our italics).

CHAPTER 10

1. It is worth noting, however, that in the Tenth Census of 1880 we found an extremely high correlation between the number of farms

recorded in a state ("farms" as defined above, chap. 3, note 2) and the number of farms above an arbitrarily chosen minimum acreage. Thus for the thirty-one states that had been included in our analysis by the end of the period, Kendall's coefficient of rank correlation between the total number of farms in a state in 1880 and the number of farms of twenty acres and over was .96. If we used a higher minimum size of fifty acres, Kendall's coefficient became .92. Corresponding coefficients of linear correlation were .996 and .987. As a further test, we limited the computation to states with adult-farm ratios at a level of median and above (as listed in table 10, note *c*). Kendall's coefficient of rank correlation then became .97 (twenty-acre minimum) and .92 (fifty-acre minimum). Using linear correlation we obtained .999 and .998.

2. *Birth Rates*, p. 153.

3. For example, where adult-farm ratios are based on farm numbers in 1880, the coefficient of linear correlation between the logarithms of the two explanatory variables postulated in the multiple regression shown above, p. 27, has the following values: 1790, .44; 1800, .47; 1810, .55; 1820, .62; 1830, .60; 1840, .71; 1850, .70.

4. The possibility of bias arising from multicollinearity seems to be greatest in the first two of these more limited cross sections and again in the last of them. For example, where adult-farm ratios are based on farm numbers in 1880, the coefficients of linear correlation between the logarithms of the two explanatory variables run as follows: 1790, .77; 1800, .81; 1810, .20; 1820, .39; 1830, .41; 1840, .31; 1850, .75.

5. "There is a downward trend in the degree of association between the increase in population density and the decline in the refined birth ratio" (*Birth Rates*, p. 166).

6. Ibid., tables 5.3 and 5.6, pp. 143 and 154. The proportion of white males over 15 years of age employed in nonagricultural pursuits in 1850 varied from 29 percent in Arkansas and Tennessee to 97 percent in California.

Index

Endnotes are indexed by number of text page where note
reference occurs.

Adult-farm ratio: defined, 19, 22n, 67n, 95; as measure of economic opportunity in agriculture, 19, 31-33, 51-52, 94, 95, 97; criteria for choosing denominators of, 20-21, 32-33; lag in estimating association with birth ratio, 21-22; association with birth ratio of a state or territory, 22-25, 26, 28-33, 49, 55-59, 64, 65-69, 68n, 69n, 95-100 passim; logarithmic transformation of, 26-28; calculation for rural populations, 39 and n; association with rural birth ratio of a state or territory, 41-42, 55-57, 97; intrastate differences of, in Virginia, 43-45; association with rural birth ratio of a county in New York State, 45-48. *See also* Population density

Age at marriage, 4, 6, 14, 17-18, 18n, 49, 52, 55, 81, 85

Age ratio. *See* Birth ratio, white refined

Alabama, 21

Albany, N.Y., 45, 47

Arkansas, 20, 100n

Bash, W. H., 82n, 92-93

Billington, R. A., 14n, 53

Birth rate. *See* Fertility

Birth ratio, white refined: defined, 3, 75; decline of, in the United States, 3, 51, 100; standardization of, 3-4, 18n, 51, 61, 67n; characteristics of levels and trends in states and territories, 4-5, 11; reliability as a measure of fertility, 4n; association with population density of a state or territory, 6-10, 16n, 22, 33; association with industrialization of a state or territory, 7-9, 94, 100; association with urbanization of a state or territory, 7-10, 9n, 25, 28-33, 39, 55n, 57-59, 59n, 63-65, 67-69, 88, 96-97, 99, 100; of urban population and association with size of place, 12, 35-36, 94, 96-97; association with adult-farm ratio of a state or territory, 12, 21, 22, 28-33, 49, 55-59, 64, 65-69, 67n, 68n, 69n, 96, 98-99, 100; of rural population and association with adult-farm ratio of a state or territory, 13, 41-42, 49, 55-57, 66-67, 67n, 97, 98; intrastate differences of, when calculated for rural population, 13, 43-48, 43n; correction of Yasuba's data of, 22n; of rural population in a state or territory, 39-41, 97; of rural population and association with adult-farm ratio of a county in New York State, 47-48, 47n; influence of internal migration on, 49-55; influence of demographic factors on, 53, 60-65, 97-98; association with sex ratio of a state or territory, 61-65, 67-69, 99; trends of, for rural populations of states and territories, 88; rural and urban

117